Black Kripple Delivers Poetry & Lyrics

*by Leroy Franklin Moore, Jr.
aka the Black Kripple*

Praise for Black Kripple Delivers Poetry & Lyrics

In the tradition of History's word warriors, Leroy Moore pens full-frontal confrontations that blast away the last nasty vestiges of Faith-based America's biases against the poor, the disarranged, and the different.

~ Wanda Coleman, Los Angeles, known as "the L.A. Blueswoman," author of many powerful books of poetry and pros.

Leroy Moore, Champion of Disabled People in the Media. Leroy Moore loves the least of us. Who is more maligned, more ignored and downtrodden than Black disabled people? Leroy's love is fierce and uncompromising. He roars like a lion on behalf of his pride: "I am here! I am worthy! My life matters!"

His message hasn't changed since we met over 20 years ago, but his influence now reaches the most remote corners of the earth, wherever Black disabled people fight to survive and thrive. Having mastered all sorts of media, he tells their stories of achievement despite towering odds and finds support for those in need, who then succeed beyond their dreams. Discovering how many early Blues artists were disabled and had to perform on the streets to eat led Leroy to chronicle Black disabled people in history – describing their inspiring lives in poetry and prose. His Krip Hop Nation is peopled with Black disabled talent over the centuries to this present moment.

The Bay View is proud to publish Leroy's work and, on Sept. 13, 2014, to have named him Champion of Disabled People in the Media on Black Media Appreciation Night. No one has done more to bring Black disabled people out of the shadows and into the sunshine of recognition, respect and revolutionary zeal for full equality than Leroy Moore.

~ Mary Ratcliff, editor of the San Francisco Bay View Newspaper

I experienced the poetry of Leroy Moore for the first time well over a decade ago and was thus imbued in the textured cadences of Krip Hop. Since then, his work has continued to epitomize societal awareness and palpable vicarious experience. His consistency and dedication to the craft are undeniably evidenced through his writings.

~ Taalam Acey, International Spoken Word Artist

In *Black Kripple Delivers Poetry & Lyrics*, Leroy Moore has gives us love songs of joy and sadness, success and failure, and hope and disappointment. His love for Disability and Blackness shows us all how to be.

Mr. Moore adds new dimensions to the rich and varied world of Black literature – he writes of the Black disabled experience of racism *and* ableism. His storytelling recounts the struggle, pain, achievement, and triumph of Black disabled people and their families. He incorporates lessons learned from slavery to hip-hop, from Harriet Tubman to Ray Charles and a long list of other Black disabled people who contributed their gifts and talents to the world.

Mr. Moore gently takes us on a ride of emotions that move us to reflect on who we are and what body/mind differences mean to each of us. His work challenges us to think about who we love and accept into our world.

Black Kripple Delivers Poetry & Lyrics is a beautiful addition to Leroy Moore's body of work as a spoken word artist, poet, and activist.

~ Jane Dunhamn, Director National Black Disability Coalition

Leroy F. Moore, Jr. writes with all the fierceness and urgency of a poet who consistently puts his body on the line. Although he reports "From the Outskirts," Leroy is unwilling to accept the label of outsider. As a "Black Disabled Man with a Big Mouth and a High I.Q." his words and his community work push his voice insistently into the center and the spotlight, which is exactly where he belongs.

His work is not about charity, tolerance, liberalism, or tokenism, his work is about liberation. From his krip hop performances to his poetry to his race and disability consulting, Leroy reminds us all to love our bodies, to trust our brilliance, to find the humor, to build community, and to keep up the fight for justice against all oppressions.

~ Aya de Leon, writer/performer of *Thieves in the Temple: The Reclaiming of Hip Hop*

"Niggahhhhhhh wid Disabilities, here, there, EVERYWHERE.....!"

Words of revolution shout at you from every inch of the new book; *Black Kripple Delivers Poetry & Lyrics.* Leroy Moore, race and disability scholar at POOR Magazine's Race, Poverty and Media Justice Institute and columnist with PoorNewsNetwork, leaps off the page at you with truth, real-ness, humour and poetic scholarship about our communities; our people and our resistance. ALL communities that have EVER been marginalized, unheard and oppressed will gain brute strength, thick activism and urgently needed scholarship from his revolutionary words and images. *Black Kripple Delivers Poetry & Lyrics* is a Poetic Revolution that canNOT Be heard or read Anywhere Else in Amerikkka.

~ Tiny aka Lisa Gray-Garcia, author of *Criminal of Poverty; Growing Up Homeless in America*

I cannot recommend it enough, *Black Kripple Delivers Poetry & Lyrics*... In 2001, I started working as a peer mental health advocate in SF. Leroy Moore who had founded an organization called Disability Advocates for Minorities (DAMO) would become my mentor, inspiration and brother in the struggle.

As we sat in city hall waiting to speak on another ridiculous law being sent out to further incarcerate and criminalize our people, most in poverty, un-housed in anguish, I would find solace in Leroy leaning into me and breaking down the jargon of these law holders ... "so, they want more money for research meaning more money going to administrators, not to the people who really need it... look out, here comes more red tape to real assistance" ... but when he got up to confront the board of supervisors and look them in the eye, the usually distracted room was always hushed ... everyone could feel the passion & fire of a visionary poet and leader. I would start chanting "Demand

More! Demand Moore!" under my breath, because i saw him as our "real mayor" as he is to me. These experiences are in part what lead me to become a founding member of The Icarus Project (TIP). Where he was gracious enough to come speak at our 5 year anniversary gathering in Oakland in '07. I feel that a culture should be gauged by how it treats it's most marginalized and if anyone can speak truth for this time it's Leroy.

Goodness, there's just so much I could say about Leroy Moore's total bad-assness! folks should also def know that he started or helped to found Krip-Hop Nation (who were early in reporting ongoing police violence/executions of POC with disabilities in the US), Sins Invalid (amazing performing arts community around DisAbility/Sexuality experiences/inter-sections and disability justice), POOR magazine/press and several other groundbreaking orgs! For me he is exactly where disAbility = diverse-Ability, living out loud how our STRENGTH is in our DIVERSITY. How black, disabled and other marginalized people are never broken people but rather always absolutely vital people. His new book should be required reading for anyone interested in life, art & justice!

~ Bonfire Madigan Shive

Front Cover by Micah Bazant

Chapter 1 Cartoon of Leroy by Deacon Burns &
 Jim Lujan

Page 4 Photo by Leroy Moore

Chapter 2 Image by DJ Quad

Page 57 Drawing by Damon Shuja Johnson

Chapter 3 Luis & Leroy by Melissa Moore

Chapter 4 Image of Leroy by Todd Herman

Page 147 Nephews and Niece by Melissa Moore

Back Cover photo of Leroy by family member

ISBN: 978-0-9860600-8-3

Poetic Matrix Press
www.poeticmatrix.com

Author Note

From Blues to Black poetry and beyond there have always been Black disabled activists, musicians, visual artists, writers and poets, however, most of the time their disability, a part of their identity, was a hush hush thing. Disability was all about overcoming and they didn't feel a sense of community or empowerment back in the day and sadly on a grand scale even today. Although we had artists like the late Cripple Clarence Lofton (March 28, 1887 - January 9, 1957) to late Soulful singers like Water Jackson (March 19, 1938 – June 20, 1983) and Robert Winters (1949-1997) to today Hip-Hop artists like MF Grimm aka Percy Carey (born 11 June 1970 -) to poets like the late Celeste White and Lynn Manning (born April 30, 1955 - Aug 3, 2015) and so on. Black disabled poets and musicians are nine times out of ten not able to wear their identities with pride as they create their work even today thus our rich history, culture and writing goes unknown to the Black community, Black scholars and the general public.

As a Black disabled journalist, researcher, poet, activist and song writer, I've always realized and wrote that we, Black disabled activists, artists, writers, poets and musicians, are and have been out there for a long time writing, singing, speaking and opening up doors to the publishing, art, music and activist world. We have been, and today in greater numbers, debunking the popular notion that has been leveled at us over and over again by others and that is, "You are not marketable and there is no audience for your work!" In institutions from schools to the music industry to entertainment, Black disabled writers, musicians, visual artists and others have been discriminated against and ripped off by others, from the ripping off of Black blind Blues artists to exhibiting, caging and displaying Black disabled people like Joice Helth (c.1756 – February 19, 1836) of Philadelphia to some of today's non-disabled Hip-Hop artists who play disability in a negative way just to get more media face time but never including real disabled Hip-Hop artists. All of the above, including ableism and racism from individuals to institutions, continues to smack Black disabled people on both cheeks constantly without being punished by our traditional Black leaders, organizations, scholars and writers for their ablest actions. This makes it very hard for Black disabled people to be proud about themselves and to come out and seek publication to rewrite and celebrate their history.

Only in the last ten years or so Black disabled people, writers, poets, visual artists, journalists, musicians and more are sharing their stories; from organizations like the National Black Disability Coalition, I.D.E.A.L. Magazine to the artwork of Curtis Blackwell. However, today there is still a lack of books on, about and written by Black disabled writers . I'm excited today to see Black disabled people taking their own creative and activist talents in their own hands and putting out music, art and books on their own through the Internet and self-publishing.

Black Kripple Delivers Poetry & Lyrics is straight up an activist/love book of original poems and song lyrics that have been written and collected for almost two decades. Many poems in this book were first published in 1999 in my chapbook by Poor Magazine's Poor Press. This book contains poetry and lyrics of songs. Most of the poems and lyrics touch on issues that Black disabled people deal with but only get a little media attention. In this book you will find true stories of discrimination like cases of police brutality, to love songs for the Black disabled community and my family; poem songs for Black disabled people in history like Curtis Mayfield, Ray Charles, Rev. Cecil Ivory, Johnnie Mae Dunson, Barbara Jordan, Harriet Tubman and many more. This book also talks back to the Black community, academic scholars and the media on why they do what they do and at the same time tries to uplift the work of Black disabled writers, musicians and others.

Acknowledgments

Lastly The Black Kripple Delivers Poetry & Lyrics is a window into my life and the people who have loved and encouraged me in my work like my sisters, Melissa Moore, Myra Moore, Pamela Juhl, brother Pike Porter, mother Lela Moore & Pat Greene, father Leroy F. Moore Sr., Poor Magazine, the San Francisco Bayview Newspaper, I.D.E.A. Magazine, Krip-Hop krew, Binkiwoi, Lady MJ, Keith Jones, Rob Da Noize Temple & supporters, Patty Berne, Sins Invalid's crew, Jane Dunhamm Founder of National Black Disability Coalition, James Tracy, Amy Hosa & Mr. G and so many more. Thanks to James Downs, Kim Shuck & John Peterson of Poetic Matrix Press!

About The Author

Leroy F. Moore, Jr. is a Black writer, poet, hip-hop \ music lover, community activist and feminist with a physical disability. He has been sharing his perspective on identity, race & disability for the last thirteen plus years. His work on race and disability got deeper in London, England where he discovered a Black Disabled Movement which led to the creation of his lecture series; "On the Outskirts: Race & Disability." Leroy F. Moore, Jr. is a consultant on Race & Disability, co/founder & community relations director of Sins Invalid, go to www.sininvalid.org to learn more. He is also the creator of Krip-Hop Nation (Hip-Hop artists with disabilities and other disabled musicians from around the world) and produced Krip-Hop Mixtape Series. With Binki Woi of Germany and Lady MJ of the UK he started what is now known as Mcees With Disabilities, an international movement.

Leroy formed one of the first organizations for people of color with disabilities in the San Francisco Bay Area that lasted five years in the late 90s. He is one of the founding members of the National Black Disability Coalition. Leroy was co-host of a radio show in San Francisco at KPOO 89.5 FM, and Berkeley at KPFA 94.1 FM. He has studied, worked and lectured in the field of race and disability concerning blues, hip-hop, and social justice issues in the United States, United Kingdom, Canada and South Africa. Leroy is currently writing a Krip-Hop book, about Hip-Hop artists with disabilities from around the world. Leroy has won many awards for his advocacy from the San Francisco Mayor's Disability Council under Willie L. Brown to the Local Hero Award in 2002 from Public Television Station, KQED in San Francisco.

Leroy has interviewed hip-hop\soul\blues\jazz artists with disabilities: the Blind Boys of Alabama, Jazz elder Jimmy Scott, Hip-Hop star Wonder Mike of the Sugar Hill Gang, DJ Quad of LA, Paraplegic MC of Chicago, Rob DA Noize Temple of New York; Hip-Hop journalists like Greg Tate, Billy Jam and Harry Allen to name a few. Leroy has a poetry CD entitled *Black Disabled Man with a Big Mouth & A High I.Q.* and has put out his second poetry CD entitled *The Black Kripple Delivers Krip Love Mixtape*. Leroy is a longtime columnist with one of the first columns on race & disability started in the early 90's at Poor Magazine in San Francisco.

Contents

Twenty Black Disabled Trivia by Leroy Moore

Black Kripple Delivers
Poetry & Lyrics

Chapter 1

Black Blind Blues To Krip-Hip-Hop: Honoring Black Disabled Musicians & Black Disabled History To Be Continued

*Baby, I still haven't gotten the shot at the proper recognition
or financial support that comes with it.
I'm still waiting for my dues and proper
respect for my talents.
7 decades of dues paid and I'm still waiting
for the highlight of my career.*

-The Late Jimmy Scott, Jazz Singer

Leroy Moore and Jimmy Scott

Krip-Hip-Hop Honoring Black Blind Blues

Verse 1
DJ Quad spinning Paul Pena
Two generation doing the tango & voguing
Spirit of Cripple Clarence Lofton floats in the eyes
Of DJ Boogie Blind

Chorus
Krip-Hip-Hop Honoring Black Blind Blues

Verse 2
Peg leg Howell pushing Paraplegic MC
To the Soul Train Music Awards
Don Cornelius let the camera catch Robert Winter's
wheelchair shine
Destination? The Music Hall of Fame yeah it's about time
Opening up coffins of Black blind Blues street musicians

Chorus
Krip-Hip-Hop Honoring Black Blind Blues

Bridge
We name ourselves Blind Blues to Krip-Hop
Can't see can't hear can't walk
We've been here, us you can't stop
Back in time and into the future no more talk talk talk
Learned from yesterday's rip offs those contracts we'll rip up

Verse 3
Tin cups full with silver dollars
Street corners are again the studios
From The Mississippi Delta to the streets of Chicago
Historical duets deaf and blind \ feeling the beat
Sho Roc with Pinnz-D & Al Hibler with Roland Kirk

Chorus
Krip-Hip-Hop Honoring Black Blind Blues

Verse 4
Today Krip-Hop put the light on pimping
From Snoop Dog to Drake
Getting paid to fake the funk
Used to be white men now everyone
Black Blind Blues taught us real talent you can't fake

Chorus
Krip-Hip-Hop Honoring Black Blind Blues

Black Blind with the Blues

Born with 20/20 vision
Father left gave no reason
Mother worked under the hot Florida sun

Brother in the tub
Can't stand up
Going down slow and he feels numb

Eyes become blurred
Can't see the face of his mother
Feels the strong bond between him and her

Now it's only him and his mother
No time for sorrow
"Be independent 'cause I might not be here tomorrow!"

House chores
Cleaning the floors
Black blind and dirt poor

Red Wing Cafe
Was his favorite place
Listening to the boogie-woogie piano play

His talents started to grow
But mom taught him all she knows
"Off to school you must go!"

Separated from his mother and home
Segregated in school
Blacks with Blacks   Girls with Girls and so on

Mother is dead and he is confused in his head
Bored at school
No home to go to

Music keeps him alive
Black blind with the blues
Town to town singing about his life

Now people call him the Genius
Pregnant with the Blues
His birth is a blessing to all of us

Little Boy of the Blues

(For the late Josh White Sr.)

Grew up on southern streets
Melody rocked him to sleep
He were the eyes for blind Bluesmen

Little Boy of Folk/Blues

Learned the tricks of the trade
Made sure that blind bluesmen got paid
He guided the best many said

Lemmon Jefferson, John Henry Arnold, Joe Taggart, Blake
All requested
This Little Boy of Folk/Blues

"Mom, I'm going on the road!
I'll send money home."
"It was for the best" mom knew "he must go"

Had to show who was boss
Because they knew the streets were mean & cold
And no place for an innocent boy

Blind Bluesmen taught what they knew
Sang songs of survival
Kept their guard up to all people

Little Boy of Folk/Blues

Got a taste of tough love
On the brink of abuse
Lived grown men's blues

Had to do
What needed to be done
by any means

Tip-toed on Jim Crow
through mosquito heat & salty snow
to clubs that he knew he was too young to go

Slept with one eye open
He was chosen
This Little Boy of Folk/Blues

No space for mistakes
Avoided streams & lakes
Blind Bluesmen walked on his pathways

Carried a lot on his shoulders
No time to play
The road made him older

Little Boy of Folk/Blues
wore men suites
to get in places where he wasn't suppose to

Money & music
is what he thought he would receive
but he got a whole lot more

Stories filled up books
Told how crooks ripped off Blind Bluesmen
Songs spin on radio without them knowing

Little Boy of Folk/Blues

Is not a boy any more
Told his son about the road
Yesterday it was the Blues today its Hip-Hop

Sat alone old and gray
Singing his own Blues
Still waiting to receive his dues

Owed To Johnnie Ma Dunson

How can I write about you
Am I too young need to learn more
I hear you "let it go son, speak the truth!"

Now I'm ready just like Langston Hughes
I'll talk my blues song on stages
Big Boss Lady still rattling cages

Chicago's wind blows
Your lyrics through Maxwell Street
Where you use to be

From cane to wheelchair
Doctors said you had a weak heart
Wouldn't survive pass fourteen

First Blues lady on the drums

Making every heart beat
Raw & gritty people got up on their feat
Record business cheated

Gave no respect
Just take take take
Were collecting cans from the streets

Listen & you'll feel her in your gut
She wolf kicking your butt
Howling & moaning can't shut her up

Obama who is your momma
She sang, "I'm a Whole Lotta of Woman"
Muddy Walters couldn't swim in her ocean

Books and books of songs
Men begging her to write
But never copyright

Got ripped off blind
Just like blind Bluesmen
Should have worked together but didn't happen

Hold it Johnnie I got to get down dirty

So evil evil can be
Got the Blues
Cause that shit was evil so evil

Johnnie wrote for Jimmy Reed
Women always behind the scenes
Pulling the strings

In 2000 Big Boss Lady appeared
Her first and only from her stomach to your ear
Deep dark Blues 60 plus years made up her career

Back then men controlled everything
Sexism in the music industry
Forced to be Big Boss Lady

Was that or nothing

Forget about the bling bling
Just write the true Blues Herstory
With the Black women & disability community

How Am I doing Big Boss Lady
She told me, "son bring it back home"
Ok ok for you out there and everywhere

Johnnie Mae told me to say
She's the mother & Grandmother of the Blues
Chicago, you got to know you hear me Chicago you got to know

The Spirit of Curtis Mayfield

Superfly floats around The Black Kripple
Told me to speak to my people
To create our own New World Order

Poet to poet
Freddie's Dead
But he knows that I know

We didn't meet on earth
Beautiful Brother Of Mine
We People Darker than Blue

Miss Black America
On the porch
With Ms. Martha

Swapping stories
Brothers & Sisters
So In Love

The Spirit of Curtis Mayfield
Told me To Get Ready
I'm Here But I'm Gone

Move On Up
And Tripping Out
All Night Long

Hey Baby
Love to Keep You in My Mind
Cause Life Is Oh So Beautiful

When he broke his neck
I was oh such a wreck
Still made music on his back

Bedroom turned into a studio
Had a message
If There is Hell Below We Are All Going To Go

At the same time
Back To Living Again
Cause The Girl I Find Stays on My Mind

I'm So Proud
Sidestepped The Pusherman
Party Party Get Down

Little Child Running Wild
Daddy shooting craps on his knees
All alone now he is Billy Jack

Black on Black
Homeless Mr. Welfare Man
Dancing with Uncle Sam

Gypsy Woman
Give Me Your Love
Between You, Baby and Me

Want to see
The Makings Of You
Woman's Got Soul

The Spirit of Curtis Mayfield
Keeps my pen flowing
And my mouth sealed

Writing what's real
Have to say
You, I still deeply feel

Love Woke Me Up This Morning

(A Walter Jackson remix)

Verse 1
Love woke me up this morning
Feeling fine oh I had you on my mind
Just watching seconds, minutes and hours go by
So I can get home to lie by your side

Chorus
Love woke me up this morning
Walter Jackson listen, when the sun's peeking
She holds me early in the a.m.
Fell asleep in her arms late in the p.m.

Verse 2
Yes woman I got you on my mind
All of my troubles are far behind
When the moon turns into the sun
She squeezes me & I know it's that time

Chorus
Love woke me up this morning
Walter Jackson listen, when the sun's peeking
She holds me early in the a.m.
Fall asleep in her arms late in the p.m.

Bridge
I melt in her hands like an M&M
All I need is she in the morning
Don't need any coffee
Because she is my alarm clock
Setting my tick tock
Wakes me gently

Verse 3
Now I'm spoiled every time I'm alone I boowhoo
Can't fall asleep can't wake up without you by my side
Baby come here, its bedtime
And every morning skies are blue just because of you

Ladies of Krip-Hop

I apologize
You've always been here
Sexism ableism Male supremacy

I realize
This is not my story to tell
Just want to be a good brother to my sisters

Shout out
To the ladies of Krip-Hop
of yesterday, today and tomorrow

Disabled women in Hip-Hop
Climbing to the top
Roxx Da Foxx breaking out of society's box

Wheelchair Sports Camp
Queer White woman wheelchair user
Bumping the beats all hands in the air

Ladies of Krip-Hop
Don't stop
Giving you love & props

Take your place
Rhyming politics in our face
Playing with a full deck with queens and aces

You gave birth
You and Mother Nature r one
We don't know how powerful u r

Raising sons & daughters
Keeping families together
Rocking the dance floor

Ladies of Krip-Hop
Learning from Lady of the Blues
Lyrics full of truths

I won't name names
Cause u know who you are
Making us shake our Krip thang

No shame in your game
This is the real deal
Take your aim

Pop pop pop
Shooting love
Changing the world with your words

She knows when to be soft and when to be hard
Holding all the cards
Rocking the world in her arms

Ladies of Krip-Hop
Don't stop
Educating Foxy Brown

Deaf and can still get down
Talk to the hand
It reads, feel our sound

Krip-Hop wants to give respect
Toni Hickman's Cripple Pretty is back
Busting out facts

The mic is in her hands
Make us bounce our heads
Feel her lyrics in our hearts

Beautiful Kripple Angels
Sing your stories
Tell us what is fake & what is real

Ladies of Krip-Hop
Don't stop
The Black Kripple giving you love & props

Look @ The Full Picture

I don't see you
I can't find you
What others done to you
Erasing you, damnit I got the Blues

I'm only a man
Trying to pay my dues
Everywhere we hear blind Blues men
But what about blind Blues women

I don't see you
I can't find you
What others done to you
Erasing you, damnit I got the Blues

I'm not your knight in shining armor
Giving what you already got, honor
Now I look at the full picture
I see you more & more

I'm only a man
Trying to pay my dues
Everywhere we hear blind Blues men
But what about blind Blues women

I'm not your knight in shining armor
Giving what you already got, honor
Now I look at the full picture
I see you more & more

Look at the full picture
I see you more and more
Look at the full picture
We see you more and more

Teddy Pendergrass Was His Name

Written by Leroy F Moore, Jr. & Professir X
Tribute to Teddy Pendergrass

Verse 1
Open the door
Get on the dance floor

We are Truly Blessed
Lying TP to rest

Spread his Love Words
Come here and Close The Door

Turn on the lights
Read about his life

Spread the love
At night with lights of candles

No matter how old you are
In life we handle

Mother's Love
Listening to TP

Getting her groove on
And lying back to a smooth song

Come Go With Me
Seeing TP working on his documentary

I Am Who I Am
Philly's Ghettos best

Breaks women's hearts
Even from a wheelchair

From Krip-Hop
To Teddy and we won't stop

Spreading his music of love
Message that life goes on

This is what we got from a Teddy Pendergrass

Verse 2

ITS 4 IN THE MORNING WAKING UP WITH
SHOULDER PAIN
YOU SAID THE MAN PASSED AWAY PENDERGRASS
IS HIS NAME

SCI HALL OF FAME LOVE TKO STUCK IN MY BRAIN
IN LIFE IT'S ALL THE SAME
WHEN HEROS DIE IT CAUSES PAIN

BUT I'M LET THIS BE AN ISPIRATION THROUGH
THIS TRAGIC TIME
RIGHT NOW I ALSO GOT THIS HAITI SITUATION ON
MY MIND

WHATS BLING
WHATS CARS
WHATS DOUGH
WHATS TRICKING

THOES THINGS ARE SMASHED
I CALLING ALL KRIP HOPPERS LEROY MOORE TOLD
ME IN ADVANCE

TO GET SANTINA, DAMON AND KAT KLAW TO
        COLLAB WITH PBU FOR THE PASSION I'M
PRAYING TO GOD LET'S ASK HIM
FOR FORGIVENESS I MISS MY SOULMATE THE LOVE
        WE SEED
LIKE TEDDY SAID
YOU GOT YOU GOT WHAT I NEED.

Cardboard Mattress

(For Staff Benda Bilili)

Music industry can you deal
Coming at u from all sides & angles
Not a token we are many
Singing stories of oppression
Love strength collaboration
The mic is in our hands
Do u understand
Used to sleep on cardboard
Staff Benda Bilili sang
Blind Blues artists on street corners
No more outside looking in
Going beyond labels & distributors
We loving ourselves and each other
Rolling around on the glass ceiling
Looking at the cracks many have made
Floating on water
Creating our own waves
Not only at sea but in the air
On the big screen
Playing ourselves
No rags to riches
We are already wealthy
Deeper than pockets
No 1 hit wonder
We are the music of Mother Nature
Thunderous claps are our contracts
No climbing standing & sleeping
On the ground
Musicians comes from the streets not studios
Points of example
Staff Benda Bilili lived in the Zoo…
Israel Vibration lived in the Bush….
Malcolm Samuel made revolution on the corner
No stars in the sky
Down with the people

On a natural high
In the mirror
Reflection of Staff Benda Bilili
Black, disabled & proud
Like me

New but old face of music
Handmade wheelchairs & instruments
Lyrics about polio & children with disabilities
Living what they're singing
CD, award, documentary
Still sleeping on cardboard
Talking to the system
Reporting the real news
Staff Benda Bilili, journalists
Like poor scholars of Poor Magazine
UN tried to puck Staff
But what goes around
Comes around
Song to turn out votes
Didn't get paid
Message still got out
Life is too short sleeping with the enemy
No! Back on cardboard in the zoological garden
Black men are you listening
Track 1 is talking to u
What u going to do?
Someday we will all make it
Truth talk by truth seekers
Are we our brother's keepers?
Holding Staff Benda Bilili
Not on a pedestal
But in our hearts, soul & mind
"Put forward what's hidden!"

Afterwards Life is All So Beautiful

Fall from grace
But the same
No camera, lights or stage

One Black the other White
A singer, the other an actor
Different life styles different backgrounds

Poverty & Wealthy
Curtom & Hollywood
1991 & 1995 spinal cords snapped

On stage & on a horse
Out of the public's eye
Two paths never intertwine

Therapy behind closed doors
Trying to get back to studio's floors
With cameras & microphones

No more Superfly Superman
Looking through the *Rear Window*
But not seeing each other

One saw inner cities
The other suburbs
Connected & separated by spinal fluid

One fought for a cure
The other spoke about *New World Order*
Singing *"Life Is Oh So Beautiful.."*

Cameras, doctors and politicians following him
While Spike Lee *"Get On The Bus"* with him
Stem Cell research social justice lyrics

Life did changed afterwards
But not a lot still acting still singing
Both disabled but oh so dissimilar

Media followed one
And let the other fade away
But when it's all done

Whatever politics you might like
My *Beautiful Brother of Mine*
Both gone from this earth
"Never forget the life we live is oh so beautiful.."

They Came on Foot:

Oaktown Blue Bay Area Black Disabled Blues

Chorus
Avotcja spoke about Oaktown Blue
Well I got my Blues
The Bay Area Black Disabled Blues

Can we talk?
Matter-Of-Fact I will talk
And you'll listen
Now give me a down and dirty Bay Area Beat

You see this is part one of a story
That is reality & ongoing unfortunately.
How Bay Area was/is rich
With Black Disabled musicians from Blues to Soul,
To Spoken Word to Hip-Hop
Names not mentioned in Bay Area music History

Yes Avotcja they came on foot
They came on foot
To the cities
To take take take

Black disabled street musicians were icons of the Blues
From the Delta to California
Not by choice but out of survival.
Do you know your history?
From Blind Willie Johnson, Brownie McGhee to Avotcja
Society told us we can't do this, can't go here, segregated
us, and kicked us out
So we, us/they made stories with guitars on street corners.

But even the Black church called it devil music
Trying to heal us
Some of them looked liked us
Working for the man
With red tape of contracts & promises

Oh Yes Avotcja they came on foot
They came on foot
To the cities
To take take take

Men in business suits sniffing around
With big microphones capturing the sounds
While Black Blind Blues street musicians starve and froze
to death on those streets
Aka Blind Willie Johnson
Read the dark eyeglasses of all those early Blues artists and
you'll understand & see.

Chorus
Why Avotcja sings Oaktown Blue
And I drop spoken word about my Blues
The Bay Area Black Disabled Blues
Avotcja spoke about Oaktown Blue
Well I got my Blues
The Bay Area Black Disabled Blues

Oh Yes Avotja they came on foot
To the cities
To take take take

Soul man on crutches
Robert Winters
Asked us to Face the Music
While he faced discrimination
In the industry

Oh Yes Avotcja they came on foot
To the cities
To take take take

Listen up
Helping to unravel
Oaktown's icons
In early West Coast Hip-Hop
Blind Joe Capers

Had one of the first
Accessible home studios
Produced Toni, Tony, Tone, Digital Underground more
Didn't get the honor that he should have got
We will correct that very soon

Who said a needle and thread is a woman's job
Malcolm Samuel sowed Black Panther's black suits
Malcolm used to speak his spoken word
From a wheelchair on Telegraph Avenue
Before the popo snatched him up

Chorus
That's why Avotcja sings Oaktown Blue
I rap about my Blues
The Bay Area Black Disabled Blues
Avotcja sings about Oaktown Blue
Well I got my Blues
The Bay Area Black Disabled Blues

Another Black disabled brother
Left his mark & tunes
Brigardo Groves, The King of the Keys
Help built the only Black radio station KPOO
He was on a mission
To teach the next generation
That music comes from within

Bridge
You got that right, Avotcja, they came on foot
To the cities
To take take take

Verse
But we are taking it back
With our songs that spotlights
The wrongs and put us on stage
To sing about Oaktown Blue and
Bay Area Black Disabled Blues

Outro
Many more to come
This is only part one
Only one song
Our history and future is long
Happy Birthday & Thank you, Avotcja
For talking about LA MUSICA MUSCIA MUSCIA
MUSCIA MUSCIA

King of The Keys

Groove me
King of The Keys
You had all the keys
Opening up all of us
To many dreams

My Black disabled brother
We were together
Music and advocacy
Changing our community

Singing Robert Winters
But you're the *Magic Man*
Yes, I understand
Disabled musicians struggle Summer, Spring,
Fall and Winter

Told us to *Face the Music*
Now I'm lovesick
By your message

Grooving in your grooves
I'm standing on my roof
Singing *"Somebody Loves you"*

King of The Keys
Unlocking the minds of the youth
In Church and in schools

God is
He took you back home
Your keys live on

I promise to put u in my book
Playing your verses and hooks
On the station you helped, KPOO
Yes today we might have the Blues

We also sing your Jazz, R&B, and Gospel
Telling all the people
About you, King of The Keys

P.S. Love you brother and I will finish that book and
continue with Krip-Hop Nation that you showed so much
interest in.

LIYANA Beauty of Disability

It's raining in Zimbabwe
Mother nature picked LIYANA
To help change the weather
Prudence leading the way

Rolling on African's sand
To Hollywood's red carpet
To shake wealthy strangers hands
LIYANA sing it

Beauty of Disability
As Prudence struts her stuff
For all Africans to see
An Oscar is not enough LIYANA wants equality

Music By Prudence
On the big screen
Seeing beauty of disability
Spreading internationally

LIYANA coming to America
Bigger than Oprah
Motherland music
We all come from Africa

Changing people's attitudes
LIYANA paid their dues
New disability point-of view
Nothing About Us Without Us

It's not only the US
Music is worldwide
Staff Benda Bilili to LIYANA
Disability Shaping the media

Like LIYANA there are many
Singing beauty of disability
Waking up the music industry
Multi-voices into one melody

Join this international choir
That's on fire
It's not you or I
It's all about we

Prudence is one point of light
Connecting to all points
Brighten up pathways
For new generation of disabled musicians

Foundation under their feet
Songs in their throats
Mics wrapped into fists
Pumping it in the midnight mist

Singing beauty of disability

Scream & shout
Let it all hang out
LIYANA making us feel proud
Living in our beauty of disability out loud

This is a celebration
Of God's creation
We are not a sin
Creating in our African skin

Breaking the myth of a super Krip
To go deeper within
LIYANA hears the beating of our hearts
The rhythms that turns our ummmmmm into lyrics

LIYANA'S songs
Tells us we are not wrong
We are the yeast in bread
And the seam that holds the thread

Feeding our people
Sitting at one table
Sewing LIYANA'S lyrics
With many tongues

Singing beauty of disability

It's raining in the desert
Mother nature picked LIYANA
To change the weather
Blossoming a new world

Braille Records

How do they do it
Can't see it
But can feel it

Ray Charles did it for the Blues
Blind DJs feeling their way to the stage
Let's go back in the early days

Odd Squad's Blind Rob Quest
Laid it down on the turn-tables & mic
"I Can't See it y'all, it's like that"

Hip-Hop, here is a test
What's the real name of DJ Boogie Blind
Blind leading the Blind all the way to the bank

Supervision has no vision
Calls himself the blind wonder of hip-hop
Like Steve Wonder is the blind wonder of R&B

The Young generation is not
Waiting for an invitation
YoungKAZZ, blind at eleven months
Dropping light & Texas lyrics on your mind

Rinessy holding
Classes on beat making
DJ TouuchTone on the radio and in the club

Let's hop over the pond
To hear B-Lite
First blind rapper in the UK

Everybody has 20\20
Politicians dancing in the gray area
While record agents bumping into each other

Blind DJs turning off the lights
Leveling the dance floor
Braille records on turntables

Boogie in the dark

Blind Willie Johnson to Kanye West

"Bush don't like Black people!"
"If I had my Way I'd Tear This Building Down!"
1918 to 2005
It's all in the music
Stop dancing
Listen to the message take action
Hip-Hop Artist Blind Bluesman
Separated by time
In the same skin
The biggest problem is the color line
On the front lines in Iraq
Left to die on rooftops

Blind Willie Johnson spoke his mind
Outside Customs House
Making a statement to federal government
No freedom of speech for a Black poor blind man
They covered their ears and shut their eyes
Woke up decades later
To hear Kanye West mixing with Ray Charles
Drifting Blues
Snooks Eaglin & Henry Butler
Traveling the Lonesome Road
Clicking their canes together where is home
This is not the yellow brick road

The blind brae taking over Crescent City
With his camera blind eyes seeing the truth
Everything and everybody gone
Surrounded by the national guard
Protecting the French Quarter
While people pinching pennies
Allen Watty, Chuck D, Michael Jackson
Join their blind blues elders with hurricane songs
This is not the Mardi Gras anthem

More like Josh White's Black protest melody
Guiding his choir of today's artists/activists
Blues, soul country to hip-hop
Designation, city halls all over this nation

The Genius in the Senate singing *"Hey Mister"*
Marvin Gay in the House asking *"What is Going On?"*
Memphis Minnie *Moaning Blues* outside of Wall Street
Brother Malcolm shooting *Paper Bullets* at the
White House
KRS One, Paris & Missy Elliot raping in the chambers of
the US Supreme Court
Fred Hampton painting the Red Cross Black
Gil-Scott Hero in front of Fox studio pulling the plug
The Revolution Will Not Be Televised
Winter in America hell freezing over
USA held for ransom but no one's coming to the rescue

Streets & Stages Covered with Crutches

Walked the streets of Watts, Helena, Chicago,
Harlem, Brooklyn & Kingston
Sang for their super
Crutches in yesterday's gutters
Before curb cuts

Signs screamed "Whites Only!"

First on streets then on stages
Generation of crutches
Entertained White audiences
Slavery and freak show's cages released stories
Sat in the kitchen with Langston Hughes

We too are America
We made the music
Your children danced to
And we marched too
Crutches lift us up through oppression

Blues, Soul, Reggae, Do Whoop and Hip-Hop
Artists on crutches traded in their tin cups
Can't read contracts
Lost their rights to their own music
Still made it onto America's cultural stages

Spotlight reveals homemade and out of date crutches
They made history in their day
Connects with today's crutches continuing the living legacy
Still not recognized by the music industry
Blues elders dying alone in nursing homes

Vernon Greene walked the streets of Watts
Cedell Davis walked the streets of Helena
Walter Jackson walked the streets of Chicago
Varetta Dillard walked the streets of Harlem

Apple, Skelly &Wiss walked the streets of Kingston
Seven sets of crutches multiplied across state &
country boarders

Decades later on street corners
Blind artists still trying to make a living
While Preechman
Sticks his crutch in the door of Hip-Hop
Can't and won't hide the obvious

Picking up yesterday's crutches from today's stages
Getting advice from Piri Thomas
While limping down these mean streets
Where Blues, Do Whoop and Hip-Hop use to be
Eire silence amplifies the clicks clumps of
Preechman's crutches

Providing a back beat in the graveyard
Where NAZ lays a rose on a tombstone
Reads 1970-2006 Hip-Hop RIP
Limping away on one crutch
Lending the other to music historians

We were here...

She is (Dedicate to Celeste V. White)

She is with us
Singing her beautiful songs

She is music to our ears
Making our hips sway to her beat

She is mother, friend, and songwriter
Teaching us how to be a healer

She is drop dead gorgeous
Her big heart is her fame making her famous

She is a proud brown skin disabled sister
Wheeling and dealing in her wheelchair

She is an angel
Watching over us

She is snow and rain
She is an icy cold drink on a hot summer day

She is tissue
Whipping away our tears

She is a band-aide
Covering our open wounds

She is with us
Morning, noon and night

She is a pair of wings
Carrying us to a higher plane

She is a spoonful of medicine
Healing our sick society

She is the law
That can't be broken

She is human
Making mistakes and correcting them

Celeste White is
Because she is within us

...adical Ray

Federal Government voted to
Rename LA Post Office to
Ray Charles Station Post Office
While we land on JFK & Reagan International
It's been a year since the Genius
Traveled beyond the clouds to the Holy land
Never again to touch down on White man's soil
Bush signed federal legislation
While sending our people off to kill or be killed for oil

"America the Beautiful... America the Free..."
Sang the man who gave birth to the Blues
Ray had a dream like Martin Luther King Jr.
Bush can't feel Ray's rhythm
Who's blind?
I asked because administrations can't see Ray's vision
"Hey Mister," Radical Ray lecturing our political leaders
Ray wanted justice not a freaking post office!

Author's Note: In July 2005 Bush signed legislation to rename a post office next to Ray Charles studio in LA the Ray Charles Station Post Office who passed away in June of 2004. Although many know Ray Charles' song, America the Beautiful, we also need to learn the Radical side of Ray that was reflected in many of his songs like Hey Mister, Mom Look What They Done to My Song, Busted and his writing in his book Brother Ray that talked about being segregated in the school for the blind and the discrimination he experienced in the Music industry. I know Ray Charles wanted justice for all of us. Don't get sidetrack by guilt gifts! Like Ray keep your eyes on the prize!!!!!!!!!!!!

Black Disabled Art History101

Sit down & listen
cause there will be a test at the end
Displaying & speaking
our history & culture
through music, art & dance

From slavery to homeland security
Black disabled artists
roots grow deep
however this garden is starving for recognition

The most famous classical pianist
in the mid to late 19th century
was a Black Blind Autistic slave
Tom Wiggins aka Blind Tom was his slave name
his master used him to make money
and left him poor and broken

Horace Pippin, the first Black Disabled self-taught painter
lost his arm in WWI
using his left arm
to prop up his right forearm
crafting his first masterpiece depicting horrors of war
Oh, the price he paid for being Black, Poor,
Self-taught & Disabled

Blues is the Black Anthem
attracts blind singers & musicians
to make a living on the streets
some made it into recording studios

Blind Willie McTell born in 1898
played on the streets of Atlanta
Blind Willie Johnson born around 1902
a street evangelist

stepmother threw lye
in young Johnson's eyes causing blindness
Johnson became the first
gospel guitarist to record

he died of pneumonia
hospital refused admittance
due to his blindness

Blind Blake & Blind Boone's
Birth dates are not known
Blind John William Boone formed
his own concert company
traveled all over the country
more than 8,000 concerts
in the USA, Canada, Europe & Mexico

The most popular Male Blues
recording artists of the twenties
was Blind Lemon Jefferson
he was also a street performer

Dance to the Blues, Rock, Jazz & Hip-Hop
Vibration under The Wild Zappers
A Black Deaf dance troupe
Feeling the rhythm
From the Motherland to Chocolate City

Listen to the Melody Heartbeat of a Black Deaf Woman
Jades fingers reads I'm a proud Black Deaf Woman

Let's travel to Jamaica
Where in the fifties Polio infected the island
Skelly, Wise & Apple are Israel Vibration
they met each other at Mona Rehabilitation Center
got kicked out cause their religious beliefs in Rasta,
homeless, poor & disabled
began to sing on the streets
now they are the Fathers of Reggae

Back to Africa tribal dancing
to the drumming, guitar strumming and singing
of Amadou & Mariam
a Blind married couple
blending Rock, Pop, Jazz & Hip Hop
with an international flavor
from Cuba to Asia & India to America

Creeping into the Hip-Hop Nation
Paraplegic MC, Fezo Da Madone & The Black Kripple
Lifting the roof of oppression that suffocates
the Hip-Hop industry
Throwing away the Bling-Bling
To create Krip-Hop politicizing our communities

Coming home to the Bay Area
to swing from Charles Curtis Blackwell & Avotcja's
jazz Poe-tree & celebrate
So get out your number two pencils for your final on
Black Disabled Art History

Krip-Soul Brothers

Soul to soul
Cane & wheelchair
Dashiki & Afros

Back in the late 70's
Krip-Soul Brothers
Black with a disability

Lomax & Galloway
Gave the black community their own way
Can't erase history

They brought out the Panthers
Remember my brothers & sisters
Dashikis & Afros you must know

Krip-Soul Brothers
We must honor
Pass it on so back to school u must go

Galloway, Chair of CIL's Black Caucus
Cause nothing about us without us
His work sometimes overshadowed

By White disabled peeps in the movement
Sister Johnnie Lacy, one of the first IL's Black Director
East Bay equaled Black disabled planet

Krip-Soul Brothers
On both sides of the Bay
Dennis Billups & Brigardo Groves

Had their own moves
At the 504 sit-ins
Both shaped the future of San Francisco

Hold up, this is not the end
So many Krip-Soul Brothers
Put their sweet & time in

From activism, counseling to music
Krip-Soul Brothers might not knew each other
From the streets to the studio

Malcolm Samuel spit Black revolutionary poetry
        from his wheelchair
Blind Joe Capers engineered Oakland's Hip-Hop sound
Brigardo Groves helped KPOO stay on the air

Krip-Soul Brothers still are around
Moore & Gray set up shop in the 90's
DAMO for krips of color, the only show in town

Advocacy & Arts straight from our hearts
We still had a lot to learn
Then came Patty Berne

Put everything on ice introduced disability justice
Race, class & GBLTQ, a gently but sharp poke like a cactus
Woke up many Krip-Soul Brothers to look at their
        own privilege

Krip-Soul Brothers & Sisters will continue to change
In our never ending book page after page
Some written and some blank

We will all age
The youth will text on what comes next
Krip-Soul Brothers & Sisters take the stage

No matter if it is Francis or Frank
Waking up our memory banks
This poem is for the youth sake

The path has been laid out
If you haven't been taught then shout out
"Where is my history, my Krip-Soul Brothers"?

A Shot Gun in His Lap

(For Rev Cecil Ivory)

He was ready
Sitting at the window in his wheelchair
They were coming

A man of peace & justice
Rev. Cecil Ivory organized his community
For racial equality

As a little Black poor boy
He played with what was there
Climbing a chestnut tree

Then snap pop
Broke his back
But jumped right back

Was bumped off a pickup
Lost used of his legs
But didn't give up

Became a Reverend
Then Rock Hill NAACP President
Led boycotts and lunch-counter sit-ins

Organized students of Friendship Junior college
The question, what happens when school year ends?
Took their place were Rock Hill Black residents

Rev. Cecil Ivory in 1961 tested Jim Crow's waters
In the sticky southern summer
Told those gathered the night before
He was determined to wheel himself into McCrory's
Park himself at the lunch counter
His reasoning, nothing wrong didn't take a stool for white
        customers

The next day Arthur Hamm wheeled Ivory into McCrory's.
A prolific letter writer, he also brought paper
Wrote down what went on word by word
Soon Assistant Police Chief and another officer arrived
instructed the manager to ask Ivory and Hamm to leave
Ivory wrote what he said then looked up to ask why

Ivory explained no need to fight
He didn't break the law
Wasn't sitting on a stool reserved for whites.

Police officer wheeled Ivory to jail
They had to get over a giant hill
Downstairs was the booking

He was locked up
Until lawyer paid bail
Jail No Bail

After NAACP paid thousands
Realized it went directly to police pockets
Jail No Bail put that practice to an end

There were nine at the time
Called the Friendship Nine led by Rev. Ivory
Serve thirty-day sentence "Jail No Bail" policy

Ivory knew they were coming
White sheets blowing in the southern night breeze
He waited with a shotgun in his lap

Daughter looking back
A beat up briefcase in her lap
Full of letters to and from U.S. Attorney General
        Robert Kennedy
Along with Rev. Ivory's stories & handwritten threats

Remembering thirty years ago
Rev. Cecil Ivory, we all should know
That's one reason I wrote this poem

Butter Knife Blues

He is smooth like butter
Some thought he played out of tune
Plucking with a butter knife
In his claw gimp hands

Poor, polio, police raid
Left him black & blue
Healing & expressing his blues
Mother's medicine

Gave him confidence
To create his own sound
CeDell Davis, Butter Knife Bluesman
Born in Helena, Arkansas

Blues journalist, Robert Palmer & Eric Clapton
Like Aretha had nothing but R.E.S.P.E.C.T. for this man

Limping to the hardest club in town
Where love was absent but fights were constant
Pop, pop two in the air
CeDell was trampled

Suspended in mid-air
Legs & arms in tractions
6 months in the hospital
Wheelchair blues with a butter knife

"You See Me Laughin'
The Last of The Hill Country Bluesmen's" DVD
CeDell talked about his life
This man is the Blues

Like Ray Charles's *"Born To Lose"*
Cedell lost his legs
But found his rhythm

Jammed with Peter Buck of REM
Blues & Rock
Guitar solo rocking the pit

Jimmy Hendrix played left handed
Gene Simmons plays with his tongue
Tony Melendez plays with his feet

Butter knife is not so strange
CeDell added his own page in music history
He wasn't afraid to put it out there
Full color picture, wheelchair & all
On the cover of his CDs

Overlooked, fame passed him by
His real name, Ellis Davis
Hear this, screech of his guitar
The hoarse of his voice

Made people cover their ears
Until they understood and were trained
To hear greatness and uniqueness
No one could copy

Disability is beauty & rhythmic
Every time you pick up a butter knife
Stop & listen

CeDell Davis's Butter Knife Blues
On every family dinner & candle light table

Chapter 2

Black & Blue: Police, State & The Abuse of People with Disabilities

"Uncle Weroy I don't like cops cause they mess with you!"

-From my Niece Ace when she was 4 years old

Once Upon A Time

This is not once upon a time ago
Fathers left a long time ago
Disabled boys want to be tough & rough
Face down & handcuff
Locked up enduring police brutality
No judge no jury
Lost in the system
Poor, disabled no food on the table

Mental illness autism hush hush
Families hiding in the bush
Were educated by Moses
Disability a part of the human fabric
Walked this earth houseless with Jesus
And many still walk the streets 24/7 with us

This is not once upon a time ago
Noose hanging from trees
Hidden fact was his disability
Waco, Texas to North Greenwood, Mississippi
Jessie to Frederick
Docking and dogging that label
The label is apart of his identity
That will never be recorded
Like his sex, race, class
Still in death he continues to pass

So how can we learn
To report disability crimes
When we don't take the time
To erase the stigma
That follows into the media
Tip-toeing around characteristics
Don't want them to stick
Open & shut case

Disability seen as a weakness
And a reason to commit suicide
No one is on his side to say it was murder

The blame is stuck on the victim
Didn't understand while he was alive
Still misrepresented in death
In the grave he still is trying to teach
His story is not his anymore
Blood pours on editor's floor
Cut up in small pieces, his family's story
Shame taints once upon a time

Since birth parents saw him as normal
Flunking out of formal education
Don't want to cripple him with the label of special education
So he continues to experience isolation
A road map to incarceration
Seen as an easy prey
Now love ones sit in church crying and praying

The story and tragedy becomes a best selling book
By someone with a Ph.D.
Who's not in his neighborhood
And hasn't talked to his multiple communities
In Black & White his identity is still not complete
Book made into a movie but his family doesn't see any money
This is poetry that is real and happens to many
Once upon a time in reality

Why Many Can't Go to Movie Theaters

*(Dedicated to Mesha, mother of Idriss Stelley,
& the parents of Ethan Saylor)*

I tried to go see *Fruitvale* but I couldn't sit still
Spirits told me to get up & go
Idriss Stelley to Ethan Saylor
Sat in those seats & got blown

Theaters hide the black & blue
In the dark crying the Blues
Just wanted to see another movie
Ethan said, *"don't touch me!"*

Now mothers can't go to movie theaters
Dealing with PTSD has to wait for the DVD
Black & White both young men had a disability
No more butter popcorn no more candy

Damon Shuja Johnson

Many say documentaries are real life
We'll never feel Oscar Grant's emotions at that moment
Can't turn back the hands of time
Love ones buried under dirt and cement

Activists & rappers say film the police
How can we film in the dark
Cell phones with flash
Catching the popo's ass

Theater massacres aren't only carried out
By individual strangers
Target only one in many
Profiling under state violence ignoring the shouts

In the dark but evidence comes to light
After all of this time
The screen becomes the frame they created
Idriss welcomes Ethan as his spirit rises

Few get on the big screen
Many more are not known
Parents still on their knees
What is next, a stamp of approval aka an Oscar from
the establishment?

After film festivals and premiers
Few parents are left with boxes of DVDs
While filmmakers move to their next project
The other parents are lucky to even get a lawsuit settlement

Before the lights go off
Check out who is not around you
Feel the spirits on the black screen
Crying, *"we need to rest we had enough!"*

Caged Goddamn Philadelphia

Nina Simone sang in 1964
I speak my spoken word in 2013
Responding to what have brought me to my knees

Down right painful
Some people are too powerful
This is beyond shameful

Locked in a cage at a young age
Stories in newspapers
Page after page

Shit now I'm full of rage
It was Mississippi Goddamn
Now it's Philadelphia Goddamn

Locked in a basement
Sleeping & eating on cold cement
No, this is not imprisonment

Taking their SSI
Abuse and neglect from family's ties
Black on black leaving open wounds & black eyes

No brotherly love
Oppression lingers around like a stormy cloud
Can't hear the cries raining out loud

From Joice Helth being displayed in an exhibit
Now four disabled adults chained up downstairs in their own shit
This country has a nasty habit

Of treating people with disabilities
Worst than animals
Behind four yellowish walls out of sight from our communities

Shit now I'm full of rage
It was Mississippi Goddamn
Now it's Philadelphia Goddamn

We don't learn
Yesterday & today it's New Mexico, San Jose, Missouri
State by state we continue to get burned

Nursing homes to group homes to our own damn home
Where can you go when home is not safe?
Goddamn Philadelphia, where is the love

Nina Simone I hear you loud and clear
I'll speak my spoken word in everybody's ear
In the winds of oppression I'll stand solid with no fear

Children to adults
Where can we lay faults?
Because this must & will come to a screeching halt

She's In Danger, Black & Blue

(For my Deaf/Disabled Sisters who are in constant danger)

Just another day
Just another case
Brutality in her face

Just walking down the street
Just sitting outside in a chair
Just running to safety

She's in danger Black & Blue

Vancouver, she was pushed over
Atlanta, she was pushed over
Tacoma, she was tased

Just another day
Just another case
Brutality in her face

LA, she was punched
Philly, she was chained up in a basement
Years later still no punishment

Just another day
Just another case
Brutality in her face

If it's not Daddy
It's her husband
Or another man in Black & Blue

Around the world the same story
She is in danger Black & Blue
Born in danger from family to her community

She is a moving red dot
Ducking bullets in every step
Black & Blue tased & shot

s not Daddy
it's her husband
Or another man in Black & Blue

Just another day
Just another case
Brutality in her face

Where is Womanhood for disabled sisters
I'm not a woman but where are the voices
For this injustice

Just another day protesting everything
Just another email petition
Just another corporate news piece that didn't mention

That she's disabled
That she's looking for protection
Cause everyday she in danger Black & Blue

Not another day
Not another case
No more brutality
We stand up with her to face her abuser face to face

Pushed & Punched

Verse 1
Smack down on the ground
All around the world
Seoul Korea, Africa, Canada & America
Not a drum, bones snapping POW POW

Chorus
Pushed & Punched
Pushed & Punched
Pushed & Punched
By who? P.O.L.I.C.E.

Verse 2
Dwight pushed out of his wheelchair
Sandy pushed to the sidewalk
Mentally disabled woman punched
What's going on here?

Chorus
Pushed & Punched
Pushed & Punched
Pushed & Punched
By who? P.O.L.I.C.E

Bridge
Got a camera
But they don't care
Investigating themselves
On video still justice is nowhere
"Get out of my way!"
No taser no gun still no respect
Tackled from the back
Teenager, Joey Wilson, out numbered out weighed
Just liked Donovan Jackson pushed & punched

Verse 3
Giving us the Blues, all over we're black & blue
Black robes playing pocket pool
Jerking off the popo
No jail pass to go

Chorus
Pushed & Punched
Pushed & Punched
Pushed & Punched
By who? P.O.L.I.C.E

Outer Verse
We are already disabled
Now trying to make us crippled
Their cards are never on the table
Who is able to stop this corrupt cycle?

Chorus
Pushed & Punched
Pushed & Punched
Pushed & Punched
Pushed & Punched
Pushed & Punched

I Am Roger Anthony

I am not Deaf but I'm disabled
I ride a bike more like a trike
I could have been shot by police
Like Roger Anthony
Thought he was drunk
Same excuse different person
Didn't have time to explain
Shot not in the leg but in his brain
I was only stopped by police
On my three-wheel bike
Popos tried to snatch me off
Black & Disabled while riding
I could be dead like Roger Anthony
Would people take a stand in my community?
Or would it be another online story
Here today gone tomorrow
Listen to Krip-Hop's Broken Bodies PBP Mixtape
Then you will find there are many Roger Anthony
With all kinds of disabilities
Killed, profiled and abused under police brutality
Disabled brown bodies outlined in red police tape
2012 Black History month
Started with a shooting of an autistic youth
Spring has sprung with the shooting of Trayvon
In 2002 it was Donovan
Years go by but this shit goes on
I am many Black disabled young men
Who fill up funeral homes every Sunday?
While preachers beg for an amen
Wiping away family's tears
But inside lies fear
Shouting but he can't hear
Parents call police for safety
Ends up in tragedy
Flavor Flav

911 is no joke
They got young boys in chokeholds
Every morning as I get on my trike
Roger Anthony cross my mind
Thinking could this be my time
As I peddle to my nine to five
Living in the shoes of many Roger Anthony

Another One Dead

Poem (For a Black Disabled young man lynched & 2 Children
with autism killed by their mothers all in one month)

Read between the lines
And you'll find
Blood mixing with black ink

Another one dead
And we all turn our heads
Strange fruit still swinging from trees

Between the lines
Hides what reporters can't find
It's not hiding its there in Black & White

Another one dead
And excuses fill headlines
Mental illness, autism… reasons to die?

Hell, call it like it is
Murder, that's what it is
From father, mother, stranger, police officer or caretaker

Happens too often
As they lay in coffins
Stories twisted on the 6 O'Clock Evening News

Like fools we refuse
To connect the dots
Set the record straight & call the shots

Another one dead
Is not a random fluke
Unarmed but tased by someone in a police suit

Too many to be an isolated case
Judges let them walk
It's like spraying mace in the family's face

Charity is not equality
Blood money is not an apology
Whose qualified to write a dead person's story?

Kids teasing
Leads to bullying
Adults not listening

Media misrepresenting
Parents overprotecting
Schools segregating

Police shooting before asking
No wonder another one dead
Can understand why there is a high suicide rate

It's the only way to escape
Blame it on his/her disability
"That's their fate!" They say

Not worth the morning newspaper
But if so then dose with out-of-date terminology
On the right hand corner of the back page

Don't let he/she be a Black person
Here comes Al Sharpton & Jessie Jackson
All about race, disability not even mentioned

How many times
People report a disabled hate crime
Offenders get off serving little or no time

Another one dead
Before the first breath
Disability, one excuse for abortions

Another one
And another one
And another one

Dead
Dead
Dead

Can't believe I'm still here
Writing & speaking loud & clear
With eyes full of tears

Hung, Shot & Assaulted

Hate hate hate
It seems like every day
State to state

I was profiled in New York
Fredrick hung in Mississippi
Disabled women assaulted in LA

Hung, Shot & Assaulted
Protect & Serve
Black & Blue shot shot shot

Wheelchair user with a knife
He was a threat to public safety
As a Black man I never feel safe

Getting hot in December
Nothing new in a new year
Brothers & sisters

Hung, Shot & Assaulted
Life halted
Break out your cell phones

Get everything on video
Sell it to ABC, NBC, and CBS
Doesn't spell justice for the victims

Budget cuts
Lead to hate
So we all bleed

Dig deep to the seed
Pull out the roots
Changing our attitudes

Things don't change
Until it happens to you
But that is way too late

Politician was shot today
Rich & poor are getting hot
Time for radical change

Hung, Shot & Assaulted
Can't see the bigger picture
When the media's frame is crocked

Don't need a band-aide
Beyond reform
We are all in this storm

Will we reach out for that hand?
After all of this still can't understand
Why disabled people are still

Hung, Shot & Assaulted

Note: According to US statistics a person with a disability is 4 to 10 times more likely to be a victim of a crime than a person without a disability. 60% of women with hearing impairments, 59% of women with visual impairments, 57% of women with learning disabilities, and 47% of women with mobility impairments will be physically abused in their lifetimes. 81% of people with psychiatric disabilities have been physically or sexually assaulted. Research consistently finds that people with substantial disabilities suffer from violent and other major crime at rates four to ten times higher than that of the general population. Estimates are that around 5 million disabled people are victims of serious crime annually in the United States. There are no figures of national rate of police brutality against people with disabilities however many recent articles say that 70% of all police shootings are people with disabilities. The October 22nd Stolen Lives Project put out a book including people with disabilities.

Disabled Profiled

(By Keith Jones & Leroy Moore)

Leroy:
Yeah I'm a Black man
Known about racially profiled
Two Black hotel workers
Same race but in my face
Disabled profiled
Making assumptions upon appearances
Blocking the entrance
Can't be race because we are both Black

Black Disabled Man
Must be a drunk
Slur speech drugging feet
Must be begging for money

Disabled profiled
Making assumptions upon appearances
Blocking the entrance
Can't be race because we are both Black

Must protect others from this bum
Got to do my job
I summed him up from across the street
Poor cripple homeless beggar

Confused, disabled and black
The fear builds
As he approaches
Looking at him like he's a roach
Firing out questions upon questions
No not racially but disabled profiled
Here in the home of ED Roberts

Disabled profiled
Making assumptions upon appearances
Blocking the entrance

Can't be race because we are both Black
Mocking my walk
Didn't read my tense body talk
Friends saw my anger,
"Mr. We're together!"

Disabled Profiled
And I'm tired
Twice in one week
Its not race it happened from Black & White

Disabled Profiled
And I'm tired
Twice in one week
Its not race it happened from Black & White

Disabled Profiled
And I'm tired

Disabled Profiled
And I'm tired

I'm so tired

Keith:
The wheelchair got no diamond in da back and no sun
roof top but I still run da scene wit a disability lean nah
what I mean and every day dat I'm speaking and try to
reach 'em cause they be lookin at me tryin to profile the
black man talking bout what happen to you damn see
there was not no gun shot matter of fact I have my own
kind of plot I have to run da block shut down because ya
tryin to hold me down laughin at the way that I talk the
way that I walk the way that I speak but ya girl likes da
way that I freak ya betta get it right man understand cp is
only part of da man I got something for the rest of yall
listen something for the best of yall ya betta sit back and
try to contemplate can you really demonstrate what it
takes to create somehin kinda great in the face of hate ....

Leroy:
Hey Keith just like you
I was triggered last week
Memories floating back
Makes this grown man weep

Paul Dunbar's mask didn't hold up
Felt like I was shot no bulletproof vest
Two days ago & I still can't rest

Memories coming back
Woowooowoo *"up against the wall*
Hahaha are you drunk can't walk?"

"No officer I'm disabled
Just coming home from work!"
"What what can't understand?"

I was triggered last week
Memories floating back
Makes this grown man weep

Beep beep
"Mr. You is out late
Can I see your ID?"

Why me
Don't feel like being a teacher
Please just let me be

Black man in a uniform
Sees me as a threat
Or a charity case

Can't look at me in my face
His mind is made up
Looking for my tin cup

I was triggered last week
Memories floating back
Makes this grown man weep

Justice Riding on Four Wheels & Brown Fist
(May Molina)

Activist in Action that was May Molina
Kept police & prisons
In check
Turning over wrongful convictions

Target on her chest
She drove between institutionalize bullets
in her wheelchair
Like Harriet Tubman, Molina led her people to freedom

Out of the prison system
And into an activist revolution
Help started an organization
For Families of the wrongly convicted & victims
of police brutality

Her community, supporters and family
Demands answers about her death in police custody
Although she had diabetes police refused medical care
Thanks to police & mainstream media her background
has been smeared

While the names of officers are invisible
Seems like we've been here, Cammerin Boyd in San Fran,
Annette Auguste in Haiti
Hey Homeland security, am I next in line?
Cause like May Molina, I'm outspoken about systematic
        oppression

I can see Molina wheeling up to the mic
at the Chicago Police Board
my Latina disabled sister
your spirit has traveled from Chicago to San Francisco
to clear my vision and to rededicate my life to your mission

Time to bring attention
to how the black & blue
abuse their authority
onto my brothers and sisters with disabilities

Forget about internal investigation
Open up politician & police closets all around the
world to the public
The community & family is the Juror & the Judge
And we have our progressive, ethnic and activist media

Mother May Molina, your wish has come true
Judgment day is here
The power structure is crumbling
and Justice is riding on four wheels & Brown fists!

(Author's note: Revolutionary Love! Rest in Peace Molina)

Respect Panthers on Wheels

Roll out the red carpet
Here comes the Queen
Regaining her thorne
Wait! Wait! Wait!
The pack turned on her

Black Panthers going gray
The human & animal Kingdom eating their elders
Malcolm Samuel, Brad Lomax, Kiilu Nyasha Queen,
Mama Khandi,
Black Panthers in their golden years
Living, Fighting & yes dying alone

Panthers roaming the streets in wheelchairs
Looking for their brothers and sisters
Caught up in police sweeps
Snatched up by homeland security
Left to die in prisons and shelters

Look how we treat our seniors
Queen Mama Khandi stripped by the state
Like X, state barged in splitting up Khandi's family
Son placed in foster care
Incarcerated because she is an activist

Came back home to find eviction notion
Section eight and disability income revoked
Same story for Malcolm Samuel in Berkeley
Sitting in his wheelchair on the avenue easy target for police
Died in prison from lack of medical care

Their stories I will continue to share
On CD, Brother Malcolm Speaks
Tore up wheelchair, slept in doorways
Talked about his days as a tailor for the Panthers
From homemade black suits to sweat shop salvation army's rags

Where is the file on Brother Brad Lomax
Brought the Black Panthers into the disability movement
Only a few knows about his work
His file is under secrecy
The Black community building for its own
Racism and capitalism ate away Lomax's goal
Today the Oakland disabled Black community still
searching for its own

Brad Lomax left out of two histories
Panthers are in every city
Let the film role capturing the beautiful revolution
of Kiilu Nyasha
We all are getting older pass this poem to someone younger
On the wheels of steel respect the panthers in your community

For Robert Johnson

Wrapped in red tape, police tape. (Got evidence on tape)
Even Stevie Wonder can see "No justice while Fox tell us
to wait"

Robert Johnson on his bike (Wait, time for me to take the
mic) Going home, police profiling, for what, just riding

It happened to me (Pulled off my bike) Thank god I wasn't
shot like Roger Anthony

We three (Black disabled men) Trying get home (Abused
by the hands of the popo)

So I holler (Black Lives Matter) The time is now not later
(Black disabled peeps let's come together)

Fill the streets & courtrooms (If you're in your bedroom
Join us on social networks) Like, share and comment

Everybody has a part in our justice (Put the system on ice)
All of that black and blue melting in a pot, cook it like red
beans and rice

Turn it up to 450 over night (Don't need a jury Cause we
knows what's right) Leaving the system burnt crisp in a
frenzy

That's what you get by ignoring my people (Watch out we
might go off the handle) The justice system we will cripple
(Do it like you do us, make it inaccessible)

Luis & Leroy

Chapter 3

Lyrically Speaking Krip Love: Affection, Sexuality &.... Delivered By The Black Kripple

"She smarter than they give her credit for survived special ed and low expectations but in certain situations when desiring that certain stimulation she's trapped by that oh you cute but I want ya friend cause ya wheelchair yo no comprehend slowly it kills her from within.."

-Fezo aka Keith Jones' song Anymore

Happy Birthday Sasha

I held you
My first nephew
Now you are the oldest

Where did time go
U, all skin & bones
Like me when I was eleven

Another birthday
I held you
Eleven years today

Schooling your brothers
Your mother my sister
Watched her grow up

She is doing her best & that's enough
Life might be rough
Today I stop & celebrate life

You are showing us the light
And a different way to learn
Now it's my turn

To listen and let you lead me
Showing all the things I don't need
You growing into a young man

Yes now I understand
Time with you I treasure
Thank god for your mother

Giving me special moments
Like today, September 12th
Sasha, you gave me more than wealth

Love is all I got to say
You give that to me every day
And I give it back today on your birthday

Krip Kissing

Verse 1
Wet & sloppy
Stiff & shaky
Have u tried Krip Kissing

Chorus
Put a little limp in your walk
Some st st st st stuttering in your talk
Pucker up for a French kripple kiss with a fat tongue

Verse 2
It takes only one kripple
To turn a regular dry peck into a juicy krip kiss
Plant one on your partner's lips

Chorus
Put a little limp in your walk
Some st st st st stuttering in your talk
Pucker up French kripple kiss with a fat tongue

Bridge
You will never be the same
Your attitudes will change
Adaptive toys oh boy
My lady likes my krip kiss
Out in public people hiss
Eyes locked in shock
Feet planted like a rock
Can't believe what they see

Verse 3
You know you want a taste
Forbidden but u can't wait
Dirty dancing while kripple kissing

Chorus
Put a little limp in your walk
Some st st st st stuttering in your talk
Pucker up for a French kripple kiss with a fat tongue

Verse 4
Staring becomes daydreaming
Taboos become fantasies fear become wanting
Anywhere anytime in private and in the public's eye
We are not shy holding kirp kissing for a long time

Sexy Blues

Verse 1
Turn off the lights & light a candle
Midnight grove & you I can handle
Straps & handcuffs I tamed a redhead
Moon & stars in our bed

Chorus
Turn on some sexy Blues
Blow your harmonica
I provide the baritone
Moans & groans, you do both

Verse 2
We made Muddy Waters
Into a thick swamp
Swinging down to the Delta
Slippery all over

Verse 3
Turn on some sexy Blues
Blow your harmonica
I provide the baritone
Moans & groans, you do both

Bridge
Making the Blues sexy & naughty
With our voices & bodies
No time for RnB
Emotional ride on her melody
Like Screaming Jay Hawkins *I Put A Spell On U*

Chorus
Turn on some sexy Blues
Blow your harmonica
I provide the baritone
Moans & groans, you do both

Verse 3
A Bluesy sexy duet
Can get you off, want a bet
Oh oh oh can't form a sentence
Cause you are reaching climax

Outer verse
Releasing our sexy Blues
All over the bedroom
Only you & I no jazzy big band
Grab your harmonica lets do it again

Little Red Riding Hood

(Fairy Tale turned Erotic)

Part One

Put the children to bed.
This story for adults only
Two souls in one journey

Grew up in our own worlds
Opposites connect
Little Red Riding Hood
Couldn't cross the tracks into the hood

Where the Black Kripple was shunned
Playing baseball alone
Walking with his walker
Girls wanted to be friends only

While Little Red Riding Hood
Staying in her shell
Wanted a bad boy to ring her bell
Nighttime sneaking out her window for the unknown

The morning dew
Brought the Black Kripple to his feet in his bedroom
Same time when gray moon turns into orange sun
All of a sudden he felt he needed to run

Bust through the doors down the road
No Little Red Riding Hood on the other side of the tracks
Just a gorgeous song constructing a bridge
Should I stay or should I go now

When the sun smiles
The Black Kripple is back in his room
Little Red Riding Hood walking to school
He can't keep up always in her shadow

Following her mother's orders
To always look forward
Eyes on her backside until she fads into the distance
He didn't know it but this walk was his morning exercise

The day came when Little Red Riding Hood
Had to move far away
The Black Kripple was too shy
To make his move lets go to part two

Part Two

The Black Kripple & Little Red Riding Hood
Share common experiences in adulthood
Disability, a thread that hooks them
Music, erasing miles of tracks keeps them dancing

Little Red Riding Hood
Saw the Black Kripple on the big screen
Like King Kong, The Black Kripple
Viewed as a monster by others but not her

Red hair with freckles
Always wanted to play in the jungle
Misread by many people
Who thought she was queer

The Black Kripple surrounded by women
But his heart was closed not open
Could not read flirtation signals
Little Red Ridding Hood dropping hints in her emails

The Black Kripple is not the big bad wolf
Couldn't get enough of Little Red Riding Hood
This is not a fairy tale, a real life love story
The Black Kripple taking Little Red Riding Hood to his family

Through the woods & across the country
Landing at the airport hearts flying high
"Little Red Riding Hood, you sure are looking good
Before we get to my brother's place I'll hold you & kiss your face

Like to get you alone if I could"
Little Red Riding Hood pulls up her hood
Wants the Black Kripple to walk through her woods
"Shhhh gonna wake up the whole neighborhood"

She don't care feeling her oats
The bed is now her boat
Ridding her own juices
While she milks the Black Kripple like a goat

That's all she wrote
To be continued but not on the page
Spotlight on the Black Kripple & Little Red Riding Hood
Although both are artists they are not on Stage

Let your mind wonder
Falling in love with the other
Turning fairy tales into fantasies of two lovers
Now that is hot & erotic

Kripple Beautiful Angel

Verse 1
I want to speak
My love is not weak
You are beautiful & strong
Singing respect to u in my song

Chorus
Beautiful Kripple Angel
Body dancing in shadows
Melting candles
Loving all of your identities

Verse 2
Beautiful Kripple Angel
Is with me 24/7
Living on earth in her haven
Wakes me up gently rocks me to sleep

Chorus
Beautiful Kripple Angel
Body dancing in shadows
Melting candles
Loving all of your identities

Bridge
You flying high above
Feeling safe in your warm embrace
Got so much love
Sprinkling magic dust all over the place
Beautiful Kripple Angel let me see your face

Verse 3
You and I are one
With me when I'm down
Lifting me with your wings
Beautiful Kripple Angel to u I'll sing

Two Peas

(For Patty B.)

We are two peas in the same pot
running around hopping from foot to foot
cause the stove is up sky high
and our lives are burning up

Disabled revolutionaries of color
trying to find our brothers and sisters
caught up in the struggle
damn we make a good couple

Two peas could be a meal
you and I are original spices
satisfying hunger all over the world
we are onions, now people are shedding tears

Our words and work is true love
just like a dove
our emotions fly high above
but our hearts are planted in grassroots

They say peas are good for the eyes
is that the reason why
we have a vision very few can see
connecting on a higher and deeper level

I'm a man and I find myself crying
she knows my tears are healing
revealing our feelings
these two peas are bonding

Two is better than one
this poem is not for her
it goes out to everyone
when we find and share our secret weapon

Royalty

(Leroy is Dreaming)

Releasing tension
opens new horizons
sun tan Brown on Ocean Blue

Legs crossed
on a sterling sliver throne
while Jessica Care Moore & Jill Scott

Feeds me Greek Olives through their words
making me thirsty
for their rhythm smoothies

My Sister, Melissa

She's been there
holding onto her identity
Cause people have tried to rob her blind
But she can't be broken

Her past has been a struggle
Searching for a place called home
with open minds and individuality
She took her vision across the country

Sunshine state was welcoming
a city that embrace differences
Gays, hippies, homeless and all races
creating a liberal pot with a tasty aroma

She shared her utopia
rescued her sisters, brother and friends
from their tiny cocoon
Like a flower she opened and blossomed

Had a glimpse of the American dream
a house, a car and her own business
brother followed in her footsteps
Independent and entrepreneurs

12 years of home daycare
became a safe place for children and animals
A dark cloud hovering over her Florence pink home
Called the Dot-Com-Boom

Tossed her in an endless cycle
ground was cracking beneath her feet
friends disappeared in her time of need
hospitalized but did not realize

The city of differences
was on her tracks ready to attack
keeping a notebook checking off her mistakes
then they struck

In court with no representation

Tarnished her reputation
months later
facing eviction
smothering her motivation

No reason to stay
Her friends had nothing to say
packed and hit the road
left behind a load of memories
enemies and material things

Fell in love on the East Coast
left a part of her heart in San Francisco
trying to mend her life together again
but will these wounds ever heal

She's a changed woman
for nine months
escaping inward
to give birth

With her son in her womb
trying to bring families together
but only she knows what's really important

So she counts the months and days
until she can walk down this path
of rebuilding with her own family
because nothing and no one can keep her down

Go sister
I'm in your corner
love will make everything better
from your big brother

Tiny with a BIG Heart

Her heart & mind is a run-a-way train
Golden Gate Bridge her back
A soldier in her steel armory

The tense
The stress
The grind

Falling on her like pouring rain

Takes a toll
She keeps on rolling
Ponytails reveal her youth

White skin, her mask
She has a rainbow beneath her costume
Her inner beauty heals the wounds of her people

The slender five-foot-something
Dashing here and there
Putting out fires

Physical vs. mental
Body vs. mind
Her big apple heart flows like rivers

She speaks bullets
That hurts & heals
Herstory don't need a publisher

Reams and reams of paper
Surrounds her
Her life's closet packed with experiences

Like Jesus she walks the streets
Her words have feet
That stomp in City Hall & through ivory walls

Her voice is Memorex
It shatters glass & demands attention
Did I mention?

Tiny's vision
Is a colorful mural
That depicts pain like Frieda Kahlo

She is one-of-a-kind
Blue oceans and skies
A tropical island in her eyes

Don't be fooled
She has her own mind
And her tongue is sharp like a steak knife

Cutting through the bureaucracy
Uncovering gold mines
A ferocious woman warrior

Tiny, bigger than the universe
She holds the world in her hands
Misread 'cause some can't understand

Following her own salsa beat
Spicy, like red beans & rice
Cool on a humid summer day in New York

Like a stork
She is carrying her babies to the nest
Dropping medicine in open mouths

Tiny is beyond time
Her language connects ancestors
To the next generation

This poem has no ending
'Cause Tiny has stories
Written on leaves that blossom every Spring

Just look around
She is beside you
Whispering revolutionary poems in your ear

⌐eautiful

(For Black disabled women)

I'm fucking gorgeous
with my brown smooth skin and my shaved head!
Oh yeah my body is slammin
with my long thin legs, firm tight butt and young breast!

Mmm mmm mmm I know I'm fine!
My green eyes stop traffic.
Mick Jaguar wish he had my lips.

High check bones, dimples and my thin eyebrows.
Yheap, I kissed myself in the mirror!
Although I'm the finest thing on this earth,
many people think I look like a freak.

I'm shocked!
They don't see my beauty!
My legs are twisted inward.
My speech is slow.

How can any man or woman pass me
without noticing how hot I am?
I should have a date every day of the week.
You don't know what you're passing up!

Madona, Janet Jackson, En Vogue & The Spice Girls
stand in line behind me!

My beauty goes deeper than what you see.
My mind is beautiful!
College and street graduate.
I'm dying for a stimulate conversation.

You can't ask for anything better!
Strong, intelligent, beautiful, independent,
Black disabled young woman.

But you can't deal with me!
You'd pass me by for what?
It's too bad you can't handle me.
Am I too much for you?
If you can't say it than you
need to stop starring at me!

I know what you're thinking!
"She is fine but............
If only..............."
But I don't need you to tell me
what I already know.

I'm beautiful from the inside out and outside in!
I'm beautiful when I drag my feet
across the street!
Everything about me is beautiful!
God damn I'm drop dead gorgeous
and you're ugly, stupid, narrow minded
and a waste of my time!!

*This poem is dedicated to all the Black disabled women who
have been over-looked by the Women's Movement, the Black
Feminist Movement, the Black Gay Movement and the
Disability Rights Movement. You're BEAUTIFUL.
Fuck that, you're Fucking Gorgeous!*

My Disabled Brother of Color

My disabled brother of color
Has it rough
Father gone, could not deal
Mother strong, has to be real

Belong to two communities
Doors slammed and locked
Shocked into reality
Has no identity

My disabled brother of color
On the streets
Dragging his feet
His eyes meet mine
And I can read his mind

Life is long, lonely and tough
If you're a disabled brother
Mother's love is not enough
Sisters want a strong, able brother

Your story and history is shunned by society
Confused by what you see on T.V.
No wonder you play down your disability
Am I the only proud disabled brother of color?

My disabled brother of color
Is angry at his brothers and sisters
"Fuck you and your pity
What's wrong, do you feel guilty!"

Living and working in a world that doesn't want me
Always under never over
Under the poverty line & pop, pop, pop under attack
My disabled brother of color is OVERWELMED

So what's the answer,
My disabled brother of color?
Are we going to go on not recognizing each other?
Let's come together
Speak our anger
And set this god damn world on fire
Cause you are my brother

ootball Father Krippled Son

He played with his dolls
He watched his game
Bang up knees
Twisted body

Football Father Krippled Son

Dreams shattered
What others said mattered
Mother took the lead
Advocated for his needs

He screamed "turn out your feet!"
Can't satisfy him tears running down his cheeks
Body caste, walker and braces
In public but everybody is silent

Football Father Krippled Son

Competed in his own way
Wheelchair soccer, track & field
Local to international
Media was there returning from Seoul Korea

Still he kept quiet nothing to say

Football Father Krippled Son

Days, years & decades go by
He saw him only a few times
Both limping trying to find words
No mom to be the buffer

Kept on losing each other's numbers
Father's Days & Birthdays pass by without a word
We are now strangers
With gray hair

Pointing the finger
At each other
As we grow older
No one is bigger

Football Father Krippled Son

That call will come
Disrupting his adult home
With feelings "I could of should of...."
In his eyes, he was already gone

Broken hearts will take to the grave

Now every year when football season begins
He wonders how many Krippled sons
Have Football fathers
This is not a game & he hopes things have changed

ier's Crush

My mother acted like a teenager
Every time he sang
From eight tracks to cassettes to CDs
And when he appeared on TV

My mother lost her mind
Forgot about the time
I remember she cried
When he was in a car crash almost took his life

She sang out loud
When she found out
He could still sing
She heard him like it was the first time

Don't know why
She never saw him live
Going to bed
As she listened to *"Turn Off the Lights"*

Now her only son
And her heartthrob
Have one thing in common
Both have a disability

My mother's heart didn't skip a beat
That might sound creepy
To me it is revolutionary
Like my mother, ladies still saw him as sexy

I hope my mother
Can finally see him
Up in heaven
I'm still smiling about my mother's crush

Time When We All Needed Was A $

(For my Nephews & Niece)

I hold my nephew's hand
He can't understand
Why I don't have a car
Asking questions about my scars

He stares at people who stare
"Uncle wroy, I love you!""
Now I'm bigger than society's Blues
The highlight is the dollar store

Four quarters in little palms
Can't stay calm
I know he'll grow up and have to work 24/7
When I'm long gone up in heaven

Hope he will remember the days
That only a dollar and love brings smiles
And his questions make adults think for a while
In your heart and mind I hope is where I'll stay

You are more important then any job
But we spend most of our days at a 9 to 5 satisfying bosses
When I pick you up from school you give me art and roses
Those four quarters in your palms are nothing compared
        to your love

The Castle of Foreplay

Once upon a time
There was a castle in the sky
Surrounded by colorful bright balloons

Only your mind
Could travel that high
I left my physical body down there

As I entered this castle in the ocean sky
Birds flew in and out of bay windows
Guiding me to the queens' master bedroom
There she was in her off white gown

The brightness of her smile
Mixed with the warmth of the sun
Made me feel moist inside
My heart double-dutched as she approached me

Barry White in my ears
She pulled the drapes and lit the candles
"Is it time to rock this castle?"
No! She took off her gown
"Oh shit!" She has Hulk Hogan's' muscles

She screamed, "are you ready to rumble?"
Damn she wants to wrestle
Fighting for my life
She pulled out a knife

And grabbed me in a headlock
Pinned me to the hardwood floor
What the fuck
My mind was in shock

Nibbled on my neck
Drawing blood with her leather whip
Whispering in my ear
"Welcome to the castle of foreplay!"

"Uhh! What!"
I didn't know what to say
Her fingers snapped
The wall collapsed into a waterbed

Then the storm began
Thunder clapped
Winds blew out the candles
Lightening lit up the castle

The bed was a floatation device
Like Gilligan I was lost at sea
I was the passenger
And she was the Captain

"Drop the anchor
Man overboard!"
I cried out but
She kept on her voyage

God! She knows how to kill the mood
My Jimmy and mind were confused
Should I go or should I stay
I don't know what to do

She pounced on me
Like a scared cat
Her nails sunk into my back
I did not have time to react

My eyes were closed shut
The colorful balloons started
To pop, pop, pop, pop
The castle fell on a white cloud

I opened my eyes
And she was back in her off white gown
Looking innocent as she kicked me out

Morning, noon and night
You can see me floating around
The castle of foreplay
Warning men on what lies inside

Image by Todd Herman

Chapter 4

Porgy Sings/Raps Today

Its not inspiring, it's not amazing, it just is!
Don't erase me!

- Leroy Moore

Porgy & Bess Krip-Hop Remix

Black Kripple love story
Porgy singing to his lady
Love against all odds

Black Kripple beggar
Took care of business
Made sure that they were together

Bess u is my woman
I loves you Porgy
Dealt with the public's pressure

Today's Porgy & Bess
Have to play chess
Filling out government boxes

Porgy was strong as an ox
Now beat down by Uncle Sam
Bess doing her best to love her man

They pass by singin',
They pass by cryin',
Always lookin'.
And they keep on movin'!

When God make cripple,
He meant him to be lonely.
Nighttime, daytime, He got to travel that lonesome road.
Nighttime, daytime, He gotta travel that lonesome road.

Summer Time and The Living is not easy
Baby is crying because she is hungry
Porgy picked up on sit & lie city policy

Can't make his money
Can't provide for his family
Existing & fighting in poverty
Bess singing and crying

My man is gone now
The Popo took him some how
Got him bowing down

Three strikes bail so high
Bess, back to the oldest occupation, selling her body
Just to get her man out of the penitentiary

I Got Plenty O' Nothin'
Don't need anything
Just give me my Porgy

Gentrification sweeping
Closed down Catfish Row
Here come those buzzards

Man & woman just working

Troubles are coming
Buzzards pack your things & fly from here
Porgy is young again look out all you politicians

It Ain't Necessarily so
What is in the Bible It Ain't Necessarily so?
Everybody, queers kripples, all races

Jump over the broom get marry be happy

Bess I want her now
Tell me the truth
Where is my girl?
Where is my Bess?

The state can't get in my way
Dragging my feet across this country
Oh Lord I'm on my way

Illegal love
Some say
Porgy & Bess came a long way

Living but not like Romeo & Juliet
Being Black Kripple & poor real day image
From 1912 to the end of time

Surviving in the saying of Fredrick Douglas
"No struggle no progress"
That is today's Porgy & Bess

The Holy Ghost of Barbara Jordan

Intro Verse
Jordan's holy ghost is our host
Singing speaking the gospel
This is for my people
Women from coast to coast

Verse 1
Big Bold & Black
She called out Richard Nixon
Lived in the closet didn't think it's a sin
GLBTQ mixed later by disability, Barbara Jordan

Chorus
She's a healer
Didn't bite her tongue
Four-wheeler still was a debater
Every word equaled Truth to power

Shout out her name

Verse 2
Fashion changes but her name remains
From blue jeans to Hijab
Dashikis to Snoods
Hip-Hop to Hoodies Choirgirls & Begirls

Come together and sing the chorus

Chorus
She's a healer
Didn't bite her tongue
Four-wheeler still was a debater
Every word equaled Truth to power

Shout out her name

Bridge
The first Black woman in TX legislature.
We all knew for sure
She would have the last word
Sponsored bills that championed the cause of Black & poor

Verse 3
Calling on my sisters
Hold the hands of each other
No more divide & conquer
Time to come together sharing power

Chorus
She's a healer
Didn't bite her tongue
Four-wheeler still was a debater
Every word equaled Truth to power

Shout out her name

Outer Verse
Taste Sweet Honey in the Rock
Barbara Jordan cracked the voting block
From politics to music
Holy ghost at work, click click freedom chains r unlocked

When Black Disabled Scholars Die

For Black Disabled Scholars & Activists who recently
passed away and for us to keep his/her work alive

He/She works in isolation
Ripples becomes waves
Spreading on the earth
For future generations

When Black Disabled Scholars/Activists Die

Who will rise
To continue to write
And fight
To keep their work in the public eye

We will all die
That is why
Life is more about we & less about I
But everything starts with one then becomes many

When Black Disabled Scholars/Activists Die

Do we, the community, take time
To learn about his or her life
Or do we just go back to our 9 to 5
We should ask why they r still not in our text books

While we read about President Nixon, the Crook
We don't need a federal holiday to pay respect
And to give back
Follow their words put them into action

When Black Disabled Scholars/Activists Die

Do we get a memorial
Time goes on
There are spider webs on their tombstones
Caught up in ivory walls their words who will own

Black disabled youth searching
No mirrors no reflection
BA MA still don't know who I am
Found I'm not alone through self-education

When Black Disabled Scholars/Activists Die

Oppression even in the grave
Still We Rise creating pathways
Broken frames mending for a picture that lies inside
Who will hang this exhibit with our assistors' names

ʲe Get Out The Way

(The Political Remix)

Move get out the way
get out the way
get out the way
Move get out the way
get out the way
get out the way
Move get out the way

Ludacris who is in the way
More like record label A&Rs
Black & Blue team up with Black robes
Who will put you behind bars

Yes say it

Move get out the way
get out the way
get out the way
Move get out the way
get out the way
get out the way
Move get out the way

I used to like it
But I was young
Then I grew up
Listen to the lyrics it made me sick

Ludacris who is in the way
Uncle Sam taking half
What do you say?
Bitch get out my way

Slapping down another oppress
While the corporate man kicking your ass
Got you selling chicken & beer
My remix you have to hear

122

Move get out the way
get out the way
get out the way
Move get out the way
get out the way
get out the way
Move get out the way

But the system wants us to fight each other
East verse West been down that road
Come on brother we can be bigger
Trying to take you back home

Oh no got u playing step n fetch on stage
Just to get paid
Your own contract u can't read
So u just sign on the last page

Back to your simple vocabulary
To tell your story
Love & Hip-Hop
ATL gentrifying the whole freakin city

Move get out the way
get out the way
get out the way
Move get out the way
get out the way
get out the way

Got a wife & daughter
But on record u call out her name
This might sound insane
But don't you know your talent is a game

Moved around on a checker board
Until the one who moves u gets bored
There goes your ass thrown away in the trash
So u keep your head up your ass

So I say
Move get out the way
get out the way
get out the way
Move get out the way
get out the way
get out the way

Ludacris you are in my way
Move get out the way
get out the way
get out the way
Move get out the way

This is my remix
Cause you are beyond being fix
So sit down & take a rest
You must learn
So bring on Dead Prez

Kraving

I want to tell you a story

Kripple boy reaching adulthood
Living in the hood no one thought he could
Busting out of societal box kicking in the mosh pit
To spit his own Hip-Hop & he shouts

Krip-Hop Krip Rock
Krip-Hop Krip Rock
Krip-Hop Krip Rock

Spraying mace in your face
Black & Blue all over you
Taking out our oppressors one by one
The state has lost Krip-Hop has won

Limp it roll it march it on down

Krip-Hop Krip Rock
Krip-Hop Krip Rock
Krip-Hop Krip Rock

Streets burning up
Occupy get out of our way
CP MS, MD everyone follow me
Freak what the politicians have to say

Click click all in your ear
No bill collector on the phone
No rent to pay
Pop pop pop Krip-Hop Krip Rock is here to stay

Krip-Hop Krip Rock

Alternative Hip-Hop Punk
Kounterclockwise
Mixing up the funk
Kaya & Deacon eye to eye

Kripple Boy Kripple man
Living on SSI but he got a plan
No wings he still can fly
On concrete banging his head shouting

Krip-Hop Krip Rock
Krip-Hop Krip Rock
Krip-Hop Krip Rock

Little Leroy of Yesterdays & Tomorrows

He was born and saw tears
Age 2 & he felt people's fears
Little Leroy another Black cripple boy
In a house filled with love & joy

One step outside the door
questioned himself he ain't sure
Left family's strength to feel his weakness
After hours he is back inside crying on the floor

Every day looking out the window
It hurts but he still wants to go
Mother wants to protect
Father says, "let him go!"

Playing T ball
with braces, walker & all
Swing swing then hit
rolls into the street and he falls

Dad holds Mom back inside the front door
Little Leroy picks himself up
No walker he is proud & pumped
For the first time he is sure

A lot of ups & downs
From Jackson Five to Ozzy Osborn
He dibbles & dabs
Watching outside of early Hip-Hop cyphers

Body, muscular puberty hits
Girls he miss waiting for his first kiss
High school crush never spoken
Yes, heart consistently broken

Examples of masculinity did't look like teenage Leroy
Wheelchair sports, track & weights
Becoming a man inside he concentrates
Body is one thing heart & mind teach us everything

Fell in love at age 40 something
Still feeling the Little Leroy
Sometimes scared & adventurous
Like his old ways & tip-toeing into new adventures

Sad to see many of tomorrow Little Leroy's
Playing T Ball
And he wants to catch them before they fall
He knows that he can only look on, watch them grow &
pray for them all

I'm Fucking Broke

My life is no Hip-Hop video
Conscious rap still don't know
I can't pertain no lights camera or action
Let me break you off something lets go

I'm Fucking Broke

Not spiting Hip-Hop more like crying the Blues
No cypher got gentrified off my corner
No Adidas I got holes in my Payless's shoes
Ray Charles sang my anthem, "Busted & I was born to lose!"

I'm Fucking Broke

Not laughing its no joke
The price of Hip-Hop culture is now out of my reach
We use to be it now we buy it
All of this paraphernalia can't afford to fall for the okie doke

My three-wheel bike is my limo
Don't look like what is on Love & Hip-Hop
At the end of the month
That is the time I'm at the lowest of my low

I'm Fucking Broke

That is for real
Hustling & dealing
Tap-dancing & jiving
For that dollar

Back then Blind Willie Johnson moaned
Today I'm hollowing
Off beat & Out of tune
Driving me to become a loon

Not spiting Hip-Hop more like crying the Blues
No cypher got gentrified off my corner
No adidas I got holes in my Payless's shoes
Ray Charles sang my anthem, "Busted & I was born to lose!"

Not even on YouTube
Under the underground can't hear a sound
So fucking broke can't even buy a rope to get out
I'm done, I'm through

Just close the coffin so like Hip-Hop I can R.I.P.

Poet Wants To Sing

Verse 1
Like Gil Scott-Heron
Turning stanzas into verses
Poems into songs

Chorus
This poet wants to sing

Verse 2
Like Jill Scott
Singer & poet wrapped in one
You make me feel creative & hot

Chorus
This poet wants to sing

Verse 3
Teach me how to keep a tune and harmonize
As I daydream starring in your eyes
Your hand on my chest controlling my breath

Bridge
Got you swinging from my poetree
On the dance floor want you to hold me
As we grind to my love song CD
Make you lovesick through my heartfelt lyrics

Chorus
This poet wants to sing

Verse 4
You, a singer me, a poet
Mixing our art like it's a drink on the rocks
Swallow it down, singer speaks and poet sings

Moan To Me

Intro
Mmmmmmmm
Mmmmmmmm

Verse 1
Moan to me no not my baby
Going back down to the Delta
In the air you hear them holla
Sweating in the southern humidity

Chorus
Black blind men on corners
Singing for their rent & dinner
Blind Willie Johnson moan to me
Wailing about Black reality

Verse 2
No lyrics no words
It's all about feelings
Free like a bird
But with no wings

Chorus
Black blind men on corners
Singing for their rent & dinner
Blind Willie Johnson moan to me
Wailing about Black reality

Bridge
Not one tear, Jim Crow fear
Michelle Alexander yeah it's still here
Let's all moan
Trying to connect with our cell phones

Verse 3
All we want is human touch
Is that asking too much?
Going back down to the Delta
News coming from the Blues, don't need media

Chorus
Black blind men on corners
Singing for their rent & dinner
Blind Willie Johnson moan to me
Wailing about Black reality

Verse 4
Blues women show Hip-Hop queens
How to get it done and work behind the scenes
Reveal to them who were really pulling the strings
On guitar and yeah we have come so far

Verse 5
Moan for me
Moan about the game we still have to play
Moan cause nothing has changed
Moan there are no words to say

Moan for me
Mmmmmmm
Mmmmmmm
Blind Willie Johnson moan to me

NWD

This goes out to all the hip-hop lovers out there!
Remember NWA, Niggers With Attitude?
Well NWD is gonna take it to the next altitude
Yeah, yeah, hell yeah

Nigger with Disability, NWD
Looking straight at you
NWD got a big fat attitude!

NWD takin over
And I'm a fighter not a lover
Nigger with Disability got a big mouth.

NWD is on the mike but you don't like
NWD don't give a fuck whatcha like.
Nigger with Disability got a high I.Q. and he is schooling you

Yeah, hell yeah
Fuck Christopher Reeves
Handiman can't handle me
Clear the stage, here comes NWD

No one can touch me
Sit down MOTHER FUCKER, You can't hang with NWD
Nigger with disability is in your way.

NWD ON TOUR
Your mouth hits the goddamn floor
NWD raw to the core

Who's next
Nigger with Disability got a gun
Watch out here comes NWD

Pop, pop boom, boom
NWD is in town
NWD with the ladies getting down

Don't fuck with NWD
Don't stare at NWD
Don't turn your back on NWD

NWD got knowledge,
Fuck a BA
NWD kick'n your BA, I mean black ass.

NWD got you run, run running
Luke skywalker or Dark Vader bring it on
Nigger with Disability got the force

NWD shaking mother earth
Earthquake, tornado and 20 below 0
NWD fuckin with Mother Nature

ABC, NBC, FOX CNN, MTV and yes BET all on NWD
Fuck Oprah
NWD taking over the media

Where is he? Where is he?
NWD in DC, on Broadway or a Paris runway
Fuck the LAPD cause NWD is the authority

NWD is too heavy for yuppies and bummpies
Ladies can't handle NWD because
S&M IS NOTHING BUT A GAME TO ME!

Nigger with Disability got a funky attitude
And you don't like….
But you ain't nothing but squirrel in my world trying to
get my chocolates nuts

NWD got BSWD, Black Sister with Disability
And yeah we getting busy
Making you d d dizzy

But you don't like
Go fly a kite
Cause NWD don't give a fuck whatcha like

If I Die Today

My remake poem of Lil Wayne's song, If I Die Today,
features Rick Rose who was supposed to be Drake
(that got his break on TV playing a student who uses a
wheelchair). Pimping people with disabilities! Read my poem!

Lil Wayne has a lil brain
What did Rick Ross say
Both gave me a headache

Hip-Hop stuck in kindergarten
Playing on a playground
Can't seem to get off your knees
Nothing but a baby

If I Die Today
The noise u call music
Would be buried with you quick

Did you kill Hip-Hop
Or sent it back to the 2nd grade
ABC 123 lyrics

But your incomplete sentences
don't make sense
You, dirty put u in a rinse

Around and around
"Big Black Nigger..." on the ground
No Nikes on your feet too big for a quickie

Rick Ross, take a stand
Krip-Hop ran u over with our pimp out electric wheelchairs
Leaving skid marks up & down your Big Black ass

Go back to jail
No one will pay your bail
Doing time so u can build up vocabulary

Maybe then you can finish writing a story
Did you sang *"remember me like John Lennon"*
Who are you, nothing but a dried up lemon

Your songs are sour please let this be your finally hour
Going back when Hip-Hop was saying something
"Got a chopper in the car.." what r you saying

I rather hear my nephew's baby talk
Then seeing grown Black men beat their chest
Give em a banana swinging from trees cause they're hunch
back can't walk

Now they are on YouTube and TV
Labels birthing Black male imagines
From Flavor Flav, Lil Jon to Lil Wayne

From Black Eye Peas to Hyphy
Naz is right Hip-Hop is dead
So *If You Die Today* apologize to 2pac

For what you did
Stripped the politics
Left us to scrape off your bubble gum

It's ok cause your flavor
Won't last
Chew u up and spite you out

Like your record deal
If I Die Today
Please for once let your words be real

Journey To Roots Coast

(With Paul M)

Verse
Across the continent
We have connected
One day
We'll meet face to face

Chorus
Calling you
I don't have the Blues
Can't you understand?
Bringing it back to the motherland

Verse
Under Krip-Hop
We will never stop
Blossoming even with clouds of oppression
Writing lyrics and creating our own music

Chorus
Calling you
I don't have the Blues
Can't you understand?
Bringing it back to the motherland

Verse
From the big screen to spotlight on stages
We are the authors filling up pages
Knowing the destination cause we're the drivers
Coming together throwing off suffocating covers

Bridge
Krip-Hop Africa tour
No either/or
Bring your whole self
Putting attitudes on the shelve
We got songs to sing books to write
The movie has a script & we are starring in it

Chorus
Calling you
I don't have the Blues
Can't you understand?
Bringing it back to the motherland

Verse
Disabled Africans and African Americans
Are setting the table
For a feast
The drum we will beat

Outer verse
Calling our brothers and sisters
One day is today
Waking up our ancestors
Teaching the young & respecting the elders

Africa Tour
Meeting us at the shore
This day is coming for sure
Under Krip-Hop we will never stop

DJ Dad Deaf Son

(For DJSUPALEE)

Verse 1
Dad mixing son feeling the beat
Small hand in big hand
Both on turntables music fuses 2 generations into 1
ASL & spoken nothing like dad & son

Chorus
DJ Dad Deaf Son
Same blood
DJ Dad Deaf Son
Same blood

Verse 2
Older younger
Grooving off the vibes of each other
Flowing bodies music like blood
Pumping through veins like a bass drum

Chorus
DJ Dad Deaf Son
Same blood
DJ Dad Deaf Son
Same blood

Bridge
Son took off into Deaf Raves
One hand on the deck other in the air doing da wave
Till death do em apart
DJ Dad Deaf Son always be connected by rhythm in the heart

Keeps em alive
As they kick
A funky mix
At the club every night

Verse 3
Hear or feel it
DJ… DJ…Dad…Dad
Deaf… Deaf… Son… Son…
Same… Same… Blood… Blood…

Chorus
DJ Dad Deaf Son
Same blood
DJ Dad Deaf Son
Same blood

Talking All That Jive

(For The Temple Dynasty!)

You jive time turkey
Talking all that jive
Pay out your royalties

Put the needle on the record
Like a broken record
Pay out your royalties, Pay out your royalties, Pay out
your royalties

Talking all that jive
Jive Records
Pay out your old IOUs

Tried to take down the Temple Dynasty
Krip-Hop Nation is in the Temple family
Revealing this story

From country to country
Jive Records talking all that jive
Discriminating against a musician with a disability

Conway & Temple made top ten hits
Didn't receive a cent
Blackmailed name taken off the list

Talking all that jive
But talk is cheap
We'll attack like pit bulls on raw meat

Jive Records
Judge will review your records
Play it backwards & forwards

Jury getting down
To Temple's music
Then came back with a verdict

Talking all that jive
"Silence in the court room!"
The heart of Jive Records going boom boom boom boom

After all these years
Judgment day will soon be here
Get you where it hurts, your pocket

Ching chang
Sounds of registers
Is music to our ears

So what do you
Want to do
Do we have to walk down this avenue

Or can we settle this
Behind close doors
Where u can keep talking all that jive

We don't care cause it'll be on your dime
Spinning Jive Records
By DJ Rob Da' Noize Temple

Jive Records
Talking all that jive
"Rob, mix it!"

Jjjj jive jive jjj jive
Rec rec rec Records
Talk talk talk talking all that that that jjj jive jive

Don't make us get physical
Going up against your temple
With Krip-Hop Nation with Rob Da' Noize Temple

We will get justice believe me
Talking all that Jive
What goes around comes around

Temple Dynasty
Singing the melody
Leroy break it down with poetry

We don't need a label
Cause we have already been labeled
The table has been flipped

Record labels playing dirty tricks under the table
No wonder they are going out of business
Listen to the music

Krip-Hop Nation, Sugar Hill Gang, Temple Dynasty
Serving justice through lyrics
We own our own & u can't stop it

So go on talk that jive
You jive time turkey
Jive Recorders roast you for our dinner

Krip-Hop

Limping & rolling to the mike
Slurring our lyrics
The concert hall goes silent

The Black Kripple
Paraplegic MC
Bird Man
Drooling our rhythms

Hip-Hop you are under arrest
Tony Tone & Fezo da MadOne
On the turntables
The Blind leading the Kripple

Spoken word from Ayisha Knight
Fingers dancing in the air
Sign language arms up high
An ocean of brown & white hands waving back & forth

Like Horace Pippin, Rob Noize Temple
Creating art at the keyboards with one arm
House, Funk, Pop, and Hip-Hop beats
Getting people up from their wheelchairs, rocking-chairs &
the electric chair

Music therapy
Healing our disabled brothers & sisters
From assaulting raps by artists
Holding the Hip-Hop industry captive

Demanding an apology
From Eminem to the Black Eyed Peas
"Lets Get Retarded"
No, Lets Get Some Disability Education

Or should we aim higher
at record companies
Or executive producers
Sadly Hip-Hop artists are only puppets on a corporate string

Verbal masturbation
What a waste of space
Krip Hip-Hop all in your face
Putting you in your place

Canes, wheelchairs & crutches
Setting off medal detectors
While we roll, limp and hop to the stage
Continuing in the shoes of NWA

N#gger with Disability, NWD that's me
Fists in the air like PE
Cause Krip Hip-Hop respects the old school
They were no fools they knew the real enemy

Today we are divided and being conquered
Spiting at each other
While Sony, RCA and Columbia pimps our talent
No wonder Jay Z is retiring

Krip Hip-Hop turning the mirror inwards
Cleaning out the closet
And what we found was
Local artists suffocating under a layer of funky dirty isms

Where is Paris and other independent labels
Krip Hip-Hop is ready to sign up
No contract between family
The community is the studio

Calling all my Krips
Invading the American Idol and MTV
Sick of seeing white perfect bodies
And hearing the same ABC stamp approve voices

Hey Russell Simmons
How about some Krip spoken word
Or some real deaf poetry
Or should we follow in the steps of Jessica Care Moore
        at Apollo

Anyway we go
Krip Hip-Hop mixing up the flow
Straight & narrow, hell no
More like crooked & wide

Watch out for Kripple Connection Productions, CCP
Videos, Books, clothing & CDs
No fuck that, we are more than consumers
So step off, listen and get politicize by Kip Hip-Hop

Nephews & Niece

Twenty Black Disabled Trivia by Leroy Moore

1) This slave rescued other slaves and brought them to freedom. Who was she? What was her disability?

2) This famous soul singer in 1997, he wrote a book called *Truly Blessed*, about his life before and after his accident. Who was?

3) This African American is the first deaf professional baseball player. Who is?

4) This Black actor is an inspirational speaker who played in *Boyz N the Hood*. Who is?

5) A 1992 comedy show, 'In Living Color', introduced the first Black disabled hero. Who is?

6) This Black amputee, 1984 Olympic skier and author was the first Director for President Clinton's Human Capital Issues on the National Economic Council. Who is?

7) DuBose Heyward's book, *PORGY*, about a Black disabled beggar, was a storyline of a Black opera. What was?

8) In 1828 or 1829, so the story is told, in free Cincinnati or down the river in slave Louisville, or maybe in Pittsburgh (or was it Baltimore?), an obscure actor named Thomas Dartmouth "Daddy" Rice came across a crippled black stablehand doing a grotesquely gimpy dance. Dartmouth "Daddy" Rice made this dance popular in minstrel shows and his name was later used as laws that separated Blacks and whites in public areas. Who was?

9) George Washington's housemaid, a Black, toothless, blind and physically disabled elderly slave was one of the first to be exhibit in a Philadelphia freak show. Who was she?

10) This Blind Black Jazz singer who sang with Duke Ellington's orchestra before having several pop hits as a solo artist. He also marched with Martin Luther King, Jr. & said, "Tho' I'm blind I can see the injustice here." Who was he?

11) He was the President of the Rock Hill NAACP and in 1961 held a "wheelchair sit-in." He rolled up to the lunch counter at McCrory in his wheelchair and asked for service, but was denied. He claimed that he did not break any laws because he never actually sat on a lunch counter seat." Who was he?

12) This famous peg leg dancer owned a country club for Black Americans in upstate New York during 1951-1987 along with his wife. Who was he?

13) She is a Black Deaf actress and has played in movies like *Barber Shop 2* and *Compensation*. Who is she?

14) This Hip-Hop artist wrote a graphic novel about his life including the story of getting shot, thus becoming a wheelchair user. Who is he? What's the title of the book?

15) He was in a car accident that left him a wheelchair user. He is now a CEO of 2ⁿᵈ Generation Records and is building an entertainment complex in Detroit, MI. He wrote a book about his life entitled, *Going Full Circle: From Life to Death to Life*. Who is he?

16) He was a Black disabled activist and Black Panther. He helped to bring the Black Panthers into the San Francisco 504 protest in 1977 at the federal building in San Francisco. It was written that his fame was revolutionary black nationalism and disability power, he had already combined them. Who was he?

17) This orgaization became the first national organization for & by Black Disabled people & their supporters. Who is?

18) This all Black Deaf Hip-Hop dance troupe is from Washington DC. Who is it?

19) This Black folk singer used to lead Black Blind Blues singers all through the south as a little boy in the early 1920's. Who was he?

20) He was one of the first Blind music producers in the Oakland, CA Hip-Hop scene back in the 80s and early 90s. He worked on the *Tony! Toni! Tone!* gold album, *Who*, and had an accessible studio in the Oakland Hills. Who was he?